British agriculture since 1945

To my father and mother

B. A. Holderness

BRITISH AGRICULTURE
SINCE 1945

Manchester
University Press

Copyright © B.A. Holderness 1985
First published 1985 by
Manchester University Press
Oxford Road, Manchester M13 9PL, U.K.
51 Washington Street, Dover, N.H. 03820, U.S.A.

British Library cataloging in publication data
Holderness, B.A.
British agriculture since 1945.
1. Agriculture—Great Britain—History
—twentieth century.
I. Title.
630′.941   S455

Library of Congress cataloguing in publication data
Holderness, B.A.
British agriculture since 1945.
Bibliography: p. 176
Includes index.
1. Agriculture—Economic aspects—Great Britain—
History—20th century. 2. Agriculture and state—
Great Britain—History—20th century. I. Title.
HD1925.H64   1984   338.1′O941   84-11254

ISBN 0-7190-1722-X *cased only*

Printed and bound in Great Britain by
Butler & Tanner Ltd, Frome and London

Contents

1 · The legacy of the war

For sixty years before the outbreak of war, British agriculture had been in the doldrums. The breezes which from time to time arose never blew long enough to propel the industry into safe latitudes. Tacking and gybing in the calm, agriculture contrived to make some headway, for there were many changes that could be adopted to lessen the depression. The versatility of agriculture is at least as significant as its rigidity, for whereas in any recession there are many who will succumb others can always be found who feel the stimulus of adversity, raise output, modify practices or initiate new techniques. Between 1880 and 1930 agriculture was beset with problems of overproduction and stagnant consumption. But these difficulties did not affect all products, and market opportunities existed, or were created, in certain branches of agriculture that had been undernourished in the years of high Victorian prosperity. Pastoral husbandry was less retracted than arable, partly because it was less buffeted by imports and partly because it could be practised with smaller inputs of labour. Where no natural protection from oversea competition existed, however, stock-keepers found life far from easy in the inter-war years: Danish bacon, New Zealand butter, Canadian cheese, American condensed milk, frozen Canterbury lamb, Argentinian beef, the litany of obstacles to profitable home production is tedious to recite. By the end of the 1920's Britain obtained 50 per cent of meat, 50 per cent of eggs and egg products, 60 per cent of cereals, 93 per cent of sugar, 97 per cent of oil seeds and 80 per cent of butter and cheese from abroad. Apart from forage crops, the only commodities of agriculture that were largely home-produced were liquid milk (95 per cent), potatoes (88 per cent) and certain fruits and vegetables, all of which were perishable or protected by high bulk and low price.

Dairying certainly expanded in the period after 1880,

1

because large opportunities existed in the marketing of liquid milk, output of which probably doubled between the 1870's and the 1930's. Equally the cultivation of fairly specialised cash crops often for sale on contract to processors, sugar refiners, maltsters, canners, preserve-makers, for instance, assisted in the rehabilitation of arable farming in some regions. But new lines of production could solve only a fraction of the problems of agriculture. Something, even before the adoption of limited producer protection in the 1930's, was achieved by innovations in ordinary agricultural practices, amending rotations, changing the balance between types of cropping or between tillage and livestock husbandry, adopting techniques to raise productivity and reduce costs. Capable farmers with some capital behind them could 'make do and mend' even on extensive corn farms, except perhaps in the most adverse conditions. The result was not the wholesale pessimism and profitlessness deplored by so many with a superficial knowledge of agriculture, but there was undeniably a distinct lowering of expectations in the industry between the beginning and end of the so-called Great Depression.

The positive achievements of the few and the considerable strides made in the technical progress of agriculture certainly did not outweigh the tribulations of the many, their lack of capital and suspicion of modernisation. After all, land did fall out of cultivation, especially after 1920, buildings were dilapidated and unrepaired, and the line which had for generations divided the predominantly pastoral western from predominantly arable eastern parts of the island moved eastwards as heavy Midland corn land tumbled down into grass again. Average farmers' incomes fell back. Even in East Anglia, not a region of small landholdings, farmers' actual incomes in the 1930's roughly equalled the earnings of semi-skilled workers, and many enterprises were run at a trading loss for several years in succession before 1935. Agriculture was an industry inhibited by low incomes and low productivity so far as the mass of those engaged in it were concerned. Not only the labourers, but even landowners, found agriculture a thankless occupation.

The impetus for change was not continuous nor coherent. The interconnected political issues of tariff protection and

THE LEGACY OF THE WAR

dearer food proved too contentious before the 1930's to permit more than tinkering at the problems. In the first world war a new interest both in planning and in the necessity of maintaining a strategic reserve brought about intervention by government that was unprecedented, since it led not only to controls over prices, profits, wages and distribution, but also to interference with the farmers' cultivation of their lands and the landlords' management of their estates. Inducements to increase the acreage under the plough, to produce commodities in the national interest, to make better use of labour at a period when available manpower was being thinned out by military service — in short, to raise the general standards of efficiency, were characteristic of war emergency policies between 1916 and 1919. They offered important lessons for administrators and agricultural experts in the second world war. However, after 1919-20 the government dismantled headlong the apparatus of agricultural support and left the agricultural interests, and above all the large body of wage labourers, vulnerable to the renewed onset of declining prices. Much of the development forced under emergency conditions was therefore transient. The allocation of tractors by the Ministry of Agriculture before 1919 probably opened a new era of mechanisation but the short-run and intermediate prognosis of this innovation was scarcely auspicious, for tractor ownership grew very slowly in the 1920's and 1930's. The cultivation of sugar beet, promoted in the war, continued profitably in the eastern counties. On the other hand, the wider effects of the ploughing campaign were short-lived and the long trend towards grass and 'dog and stick' farming resumed in the 1920's and accelerated early in the 1930's.

The abandonment of agriculture *after* the government had passed the Corn Production Act of 1920, which made some provision for continued support of arable producers, was regarded by agriculturists as a betrayal. The retreat was certainly caused by immediate financial problems as the UK entered a period of acute recession. It was part of a general retrenchment in public spending common in all such times. Governments, however, did not wholly neglect agriculture thereafter. Certain limited measures of support were enacted in the 1920's to ease specific pressure points, the Agricultural

3

Credit Act of 1928 and the legislation de-rating agricultural land, also in 1928, being good examples. Many of the difficulties of agriculture were thought not to be essentially agricultural; they related to rates, tithes and the problems arising out of a long-term decline in the bilateral economic connection of landlord and tenant. An especially contentious issue was the relationship between farmers and labourers, since the latter had been badly stricken by the slump of 1921-22 when farmers transferred a considerable part of their new burdens upon the shoulders of their work force. The Labour government of 1924 attempted to rectify this inequity by setting up county wage boards to fix rates of pay, but in the circumstances there was little room for more than a modest improvement in real wages. The world-wide depression of 1930–33 precipitated a more fundamental intervention by government. The problem of overproduction had been chronic for a generation; it then became acute, partly because production around the world was particularly high about 1930 and partly because consumption, not buoyant in the 1920's, declined even further in the slump. It was no part of the policy of the National government to introduce direct controls over production and distribution. Tariff protection was a different matter, but the safeguarding of British agriculture was not easy when so many imports came from the Empire. Imperial preference and a limited number of bilateral commercial agreements with countries in some way dependent upon the United Kingdom made tariff protection a formal rather than a real instrument of agricultural policy in the 1930's. On the other hand, commercial policy did confer some advantages, since imports were regulated more effectively, dumping was largely eliminated and orderly markets at home became more normal, but the prices of commodities that enjoyed no natural protection were seldom determined by British producers or consumers.

What the government of the 1930's attempted to do on the home front was to encourage self-help among producers. The nub of the problem was thought to be marketing, not production. Hence the characteristic but incomplete innovation of the Marketing Boards, which were not instruments of State control, nor part of a process of 'nationalisation'. They were set up as producer-directed associations with powers to regulate supply that might result in the formation of monopsonies that were not prescribed by legislation. Only for sugar beet was a thoroughgoing State monopoly established. For many agricultural commodities little practical was done, usually because it was too difficult either to control supply or to organise the producers. The only extensive system of financial support was laid out in the Wheat Act of 1932, which provided for a 'standard guaranteed price' in the form of a deficiency payment to supplement actual market prices. The results were mixed. After 1933 prices on the market rose, almost doubling between 1933 and 1936, which reduced government expenditure on subsidies, but the acreage also rose and the government's target of production, 27 million cwt, was exceeded every year after 1933. In this revival, commercial dipomacy played a not inconsiderable part. The International Wheat Agreement of 1934 really was effective in regulating the international markets for this most extensively traded of agricultural commodities. Other subsidies were placed on vulnerable commodities, though with less obvious success: the Cattle Industry (Emergency Provisions) Act of 1934 was in force for three years and cost the Exchequer £11·4 million; its successor, the Livestock Industry Act of 1937, changed the basis of the subsidy, so as to reduce the Treasury commitment, by diverting import duties to the support of domestic producers. It was hardly in operation before the coming of war changed the perspective of strategic planning in agriculture.

There was a small but significant recovery from 1933 until the outbreak of the war. In the ten years after 1924 agricultural output barely changed, tending to decline rather than to increase. Thereafter growth averaged 2 or 3 per cent per annum until 1940, which was favourable but could not compare with the rapid expansion of the 1940's. Thus the share of agriculture in the distribution of gross national product, according to two Censuses of Production, rose from 3·9 per cent, or £175 million, in 1935 to 6·2 per cent, or £691 million, in 1949. The most potent influence in this transformation was the second world war.

Late in the 1930's the government began to become anxious about the state of the country's food resources, since for certain products — sugar, oils, fats, butter, wheat and flour — dependence upon oversea suppliers still exceeded 85 per cent. In June 1939 the Agricultural Development Act provided a subsidy of £2 per acre for ploughing up permanent grass. The ploughing campaign became more insistent afterwards but the commitment of policy from the outset of the emergency had been to enlarge the area under tillage. The result was an increase in the acreage under the plough of about 50 per cent, spread fairly evenly among cereals and roots. Most types of livestock were discouraged; sheep and lambs fell from 26 million to 19½ million and poultry from 64 million to 45 million during the war. A modest increase in cattle numbers, from 8 million to 8·7 million, was permitted, in order to increase the output of milk. This plan owed much to experience in the first world war, since food science had long decreed that human nutrition could be maximised by concentrating upon starch-based arable crops at the expense of protein-rich pastoral produce because the energy output per acre was very much greater when land was in tillage than under grassland regimes. The emphasis upon arable commodities, however, had other advantages. Animals competed with humans for foodstuffs. Livestock husbandry had long been dependent upon foreign supplies of cereals and oils for fodder, but both the costs of imports and the scarcity of shipping space made the trade unpopular with government. Some diversion of home production to feed necessary livestock was authorised, but the compounders and feed millers found wartime allocations parsimonious and were forced to experiment with many unusual ingredients to keep their rollers grinding. After 1941 Lend Lease enabled the government to import feeding stuffs when necessary without too much anxiety about their cost. Shipping space, however, remained scarce and animal feeds had a low priority. Thus the purpose of the government was to reduce dependence upon imports in the feeding of the people, which meant inevitably a heavy emphasis upon arable produce. The steady improvement in nutrition of the 1930's was not allowed to fall back in the 1940's and with a better distribution of foodstuffs the people at large were no worse nourished, however tedious their diet, in spite of declining imports. By the end of the war the United Kingdom was able to supply almost half the food formerly provided by imports, and home production of food, in terms of energy values, had risen by at least 70 per cent.

This was achieved by a considerable increase of yields despite the marginal nature of much new ploughed land. There was moreover only a small increase in effective labour supply, for although numbers were allowed to rise substantially the majority of newcomers was casual or female. Mechanisation went a good deal further than in the first world war: several new kinds of implements were made available either as imports or from home manufacturers; tractors increased almost threefold, cultivators and milking machines by about 75 per cent, self-binders by 10 per cent. Altogether mechanical horsepower increased by 150 per cent.

More strikingly the application of inorganic fertilisers approximately doubled. This was vital for the success of the ploughing campaign and could, in simply agricultural terms, have been very much greater. But many fertilisers and the raw materials used in their manufacture had to be imported. They were therefore allocated quite sparingly, not least also because the fabrication of inorganics was expensive of fuel and some of the chemical works had been converted to munitions.

Allocation is the key word in the wartime history of agriculture. Since virtually all agricultural commodities, inputs and outputs, were subject to direct control, price regulation and quality checks, exercised either by the Ministry of Agriculture or by the Ministry of Food, the old landmarks in marketing became blurred. On the other hand much of the *agricultural* policy of the government was administered locally by County War Agricultural Committees on which spokesmen for the industry were numerous. Leading farmers were especially influential, since many of the decisions made by the 'War Ags' were technical, relating to land use, the allocation of machinery, labour and scarce materials. The powers of the committees included the right to supervise operations on holdings not performing to their standards of satisfaction and, if necessary, to sequestrate farms or estates when other measures failed. Dragooning farmers into acquiescence in policies framed to serve a wider national interest was not especially characteristic of government agencies during the war, for government needed co-operation from producers. Inducements were rather more successful than injunctions. Grants and subsidies were offered for a wide range of improvements to encourage underdrainage, liming and land reclamation, to support hill farmers in their cattle and sheep enterprises and to promote cultivation of wheat and potatoes. In addition loans were made available for a large number of approved projects or requisites. The result was that farmers, or at least those of them who formed opinion, became willing, even enthusiastic adjutants of intervention, since not only did guaranteed markets increase their profits but government liberality also seemed to offer the promise of unheard-of stability. The co-operativeness of farmers was not superficial, since they acknowledged that the government was putting into practice what many of them had hoped to see in the 1920's, but it was not altruistic. Much evasion of controls and sanctions took place in the countryside, not only because government direction of the agricultural trades was irksome, but also because profit margins outside the official economy were usually much greater. In some ways these evasions became more marked after the return of peace. It is, however, impossible to measure the size of the black market in foodstuffs in the 1940's.

The social bearings of agriculture changed during the war partly as a result of the influence of military service. Agriculture was a reserved occupation but it was not possible to impede voluntary enlistment and as the peak of demand for military manpower was reached in 1943-44 many workers in certain reserved occupations were conscripted and replaced by women or less fit men. The impact was temporary and men were quickly reassimilated into agriculture after demobilisation. Even mechanisation was less thoroughgoing than it might have been because post-war shortages of materials and fuel and the discouragement of manufactured imports held up progress for some years. Indeed, attention was so concentrated upon food production and distribution in the war years that adjustments to the social structure of agriculture were not encouraged unless they followed directly from the policies adopted by government. An obvious change occurred with the restoration of widespread profitability. A steady inflation, especially the controlled increase of farmers' commodity prices, fertilised agricultural prosperity. Landowners, farmers and workers all benefited. Rents and wages were both controlled, which meant that they were kept within the confines of general inflationary pressures, but by contrast with pre-war conditions the results were satisfactory. There was, however, one problem. Wages and rents were normally fixed with reference to the retail price index; rents, indeed, were sometimes determined upon criteria which favoured the food-producing landholder before the *rentier* landowner. In both cases the farmers tended to succeed better than the others, owing to the superior efficiency in lobbying of the National Farmers' Union.

Agricultural prices, which determined prosperity in the industry, rose three times as much as the official cost of living between 1939 and 1945. (Net farm receipts rose very much faster during the war than other incomes.) Much of the inflation occurred before 1942. It encouraged farmers to spend, to buy what they could for consumption or investment and especially to acquire land. It also led to a substantial increase in their cash balances which were available for investment in the future. The war was one of the more important staging points on the road to agricultural owner-occupancy in the United Kingdom. This tendency was not especially favoured by the government, which preferred to increase the security of tenure for landholders. The Agricultural Tenure Act of 1941 was seen by some landlords as a disincentive to estate management and probably therefore caused some sales of rented land. On the other hand the market was not particularly favourable to sellers and no wholesale dispossession of *rentiers* took place in the war years.

The legacy of the war for agriculture can be divided into three. First was the restoration of prosperity after seventy years becalmed. The effects were impressive to politicians and agriculturists alike, for, within the constraints of financial and material shortages controlled by the central government, farmers' incomes, the earnings of labour and the receipts of landowners all rose sufficiently to stimulate demand or savings. Prosperity, although greatly to the advantage of the producers, did not result in a frontal assault upon the consumers' living standards, because much of the farmers' new affluence was financed by government. Agriculture succeeded in delivering a larger volume of output and in reducing dependence upon oversea supplies without forcing up retail prices to unbearable levels. The second lesson for post-war planners was the relative success of intervention and especially the co-operativeness of all parties in promoting the production drive. The good feelings which developed between the Ministry and the National Farmers' Union, the tendency to defer many critical decisions at local level to practising farmers and the advantages that farmers obtained from the corporative approach to policy-making made intervention attractive to the producers, who emerged by 1945 as the dominant voice in negotiations. In the war the scale of the emergency justified easy acquiescence in the demands of farmers. It was probably too lax a regime for post-war bargaining to serve the best interests of an austere peace, but the consensus within the industry was too valuable politically to be broken by unilateral retrenchment on the part of government before the 1950's. Thirdly, the war economy laid the foundations of the great expansion and technical advance of agriculture during the following decades. This was partly the direct consequence of rehabilitating the old arable or mixed husbandry of the south and east, for that was the forcing ground of the most far-reaching innovations in technique. Arable farmers, no doubt because they have had more money to spend, have formed the advance-guard of both scientific and managerial progress in Britain. They gained most from the war and continued to do well in post-war adjustments in husbandry and the system of financial support. But the very considerable transfer of money from government to agriculture to promote capital improvements and to subsidise fertilisation of the soil, together with public support for research and development, equally fostered long-run progress; indeed, it is arguable that wartime investment by government bore fruit only after the war was safely over. This result, however, was in itself of vital importance. In the years following the war import saving was equally urgent, and the achievements of agriculture in raising aggregate output by the end of hostilities could be exploited further to ward off starvation in the later 1940's. Had agriculture not been mobilised so successfully in the war, or had it been disturbed by extensive physical damage or hindered by severe shortages of capital goods and manpower in the interests of military priorities, the industry's ability to meet government targets of even more self-sufficiency after 1946 would have been gravely impaired. Britons may have been hungry in 1947 but none died of starvation in that dire winter.

2 · The role of government, 1945-72

The history of British agriculture since the second world war has been inextricably bound up with government. Even the vocabulary of the industry has become increasingly bureaucratic. Much of the time spent by farmers, or at least by those who act in their interests, is devoted to negotiation, to the interpretation of policy or to the administration of measures imposed upon them. Intervention has been a fact of life in agriculture since 1940, but in the formulation and application of policies the role of government has not remained changeless. Indeed, given their commitment to protection of the industry, governments have not always pursued consistent objectives in subsidising production. Before 1973, when the United Kingdom acceded to the Common Market, we can discern three phases in the evolution of policy. The turning points cannot be fixed in particular years. Amendment of current practices, even when it was seen to be necessary by Ministers, could be made only after negotiation or, often, in the teeth of fierce opposition. Thus a change of trend sometimes took two or three years to be set. One problem was that the 1947 Agriculture Act acquired a monumental significance, not so much for what it contained as for what it represented as the token of a government promise to look after agriculture. The premise of permanent support for agriculture has for over forty years been bipartisan. Why it should have been so important to both Labour and Conservative governments to reassure farmers that they would not be sacrificed on the altar of cheap food as they believed they had been in the 'great betrayal' of 1920 is an interesting question. Remembering the lessons of the war, almost everyone was convinced of the strategic importance of a successful agriculture; many were interested in autarky and in the social amelioration of a rundown countryside. But there was also a political calculation; a widespread belief in the 1950's and 1960's that the farmers' vote was important was apparently confirmed by the existence of several rural marginal seats within the reach of Labour and not fixed upon the Tories. The 1947 Act touched upon the farmers' fears, and after 1951 the Conservative Minister, Sir Thomas Dugdale, did much to reassure them of continuing Tory interest in agricultural subvention. Farmers in return vented their fury upon Ministers from both parties.

The 1947 Agriculture Act marked the beginning of the first post-war stage in agricultural policy. The structure erected by Tom Williams, Minister of Agriculture from 1945 to 1951, endured more or less intact until after the Korean War. Between 1953 and 1957 the government initiated a less *dirigiste* pattern of intervention which lasted until the early 1960's. Though some of the ideas were inherited from the previous government, the new Labour administration in 1964 placed its stamp upon a plan of structural reform that promised more than it achieved, but which certainly reached back beyond the liberalising measures of Heathcote Amory and Hare in the late 1950's. With the arrival of the Heath government, determination to gain access to the Common Market influenced agricultural policy well before 1973, so that the whole of the 1970's can be seen as an era of transition.

These stages of policy-making are probably drawn too broadly. Changes of direction have often been less clearly signalled. The Annual Review, for example, has reflected immediate problems as often as long-term plans. Moreover, although agriculture has enjoyed a large measure of financial indulgence, it has been necessary from time to time for the Treasury to override spending plans during the recurrent 'stop' phases of economic management after 1955. Certain political events, too, probably influenced policy, as when the result of the Torrington by-election in 1958 persuaded the Conservatives to rethink their ideas about the problems of marginal upland farmers.

The 1947 Act stated that the object of policy 'is to promote a stable and efficient industry capable of producing such part of the nation's food as in the national interest it is desirable to produce in the United Kingdom and to produce it at minimum prices consistent with proper remuneration and living conditions for farmers and workers in agriculture and

13

with an adequate return on capital invested'. The provisions of the Act were set out in two parts, one concerned with the determination of prices and production, the other with methods of increasing efficiency and reforming the structure of agriculture.

Part I provided that the Minister of Agriculture should produce an annual review of the industry. This was intended to supply a report of conditions and a forecast of trends for the coming year, undertaken in consultation with producers' representatives. It was not an innovation; the Ministry had conceded that some such annual statement was necessary to reassure farmers in 1943, but the practice had hitherto been informal. Since the government remained the principal purchaser of all agricultural produce and allocated most materials to the farmers, its monopoly had to be tempered by negotiation.

For the most part, the 1947 Act proposed to continue the wartime practice of direct purchase and allocation into the foreseeable future in order to conserve scarce resources. The review would state price levels for the year ahead. These would be guaranteed by the Ministry and an assured market provided for all the commodities listed in the Act as appropriate for protection. Almost all products, except horticultural produce, were enumerated and the Act made provision for future changes by empowering the Minister to add new commodities when necessary. The annual review could be supplemented by special reviews to take account of extraordinary economic circumstances.

The review thus became an instrument both of planning and of regulation. The Act, however, went further. It left virtually intact the responsibility of the government and its power to adjust the subsidisation of agriculture inherited from the war. But experience had suggested that the simple subvention of farm production by fixing the prices of approved commodities was rather inflexible. Guarantees could be given in the form of an acreage payment or a producer's subsidy. Moreover, since the Ministry did not wish to be inundated with produce that glutted the market, the Act empowered government to set limits for production either by determining output or by allocating acreage (and/or seed) for particular commodities.

Allowing too rapid an expansion of production could impose a strain upon resources of capital or other inputs. Nevertheless, it is true that in the conditions of 1947, and for several years thereafter, the Ministry was more interested in maximising physical production than in fine-tuning agriculture, but it was already evident that, to increase food supplies from domestic sources permanently, important structural changes were necessary.

Agricultural practices were often inadequate to meet the needs of a hungry people. Farmers had to be encouraged to adopt new methods, to follow more profitable lines of business, to apply new fertilisers or strains of seed and to convert land to new uses. It was not even necessarily true that wartime expansion was appropriate for peacetime conditions. A combination of coercion and incentive was proposed. Improvement grants were to be offered for a variety of uses. Particularly important were the subsidisation of fertilisers, especially nitrates and phosphates, and grants for underdrainage, the application of lime, conversion to tillage and the provision of new buildings. At the same time the threat of enforcement in order to bring recalcitrant or incompetent farmers into line was restated in the establishment of County Agricultural Committees to take over where the old War Ags had left off. A different statute embodied a new National Agricultural Advisory Service. The Labour government, faced with a choice of restoring the service, together with new functions developed during the war, to the county councils or of centralising the institution under the Ministry, preferred the latter option. The NAAS was intended essentially to respond to farmer's requests for technical assistance, but could in certain circumstances initiate improvements. The advisory service was involved with the County Agricultural Committees in correcting errant practices, but also acted as the channel through which farmers' applications for grants were submitted for approval. The Conservatives were not happy with the commingling of advisory and regulatory functions in NAAS, but the incompatibility of the two roles was not otherwise immediately apparent.

The policy which Tom Williams formulated in 1946–47 was not notably consistent, but the lack of clarity in detail tended to enlarge the field of action of the Minister and his civil servants. It also provided scope for negotiation with interested parties, especially the farmers, who found that, with a sympathetic Minister, they could obtain a large proportion of their demands at the time of the annual review. A *rapport* developed between Williams, and his successor, Dugdale, and James Turner of the NFU which was in itself one of the most remarkable portents of the age. Nevertheless, a high degree of satisfaction within the industry did not necessarily justify the policies on economic grounds. The first premise of the legislation posed a dilemma. The general intention to increase food production in order both to improve the nutrition of the people and to make substantial import savings was prudent, but the attempt to maintain cheap food at the same time as farmers' living standards were to be raised implied a much higher level of government spending upon agriculture than had ever been contemplated in peacetime. Autarky and cheap food were not inevitably contradictory, but the difficulties of driving two captious horses in a single team were borne out as the journey out of austerity proceeded.

But in 1947 the production of even more food than had been achieved in wartime was imperative. The dollar crisis that bedevilled British economic policy for years after the end of Lend-Lease was in a particularly acute phase in 1947. Quite apart from the overriding need to save dollars by reducing all imports, the disruption of world agriculture, chiefly caused by the war, compelled importers (i.e. the government) to rely more heavily upon the dollar area than had been the case in the 1930's. There was, therefore, a double disadvantage in dependence upon imports after the war, which was compounded by the relatively high prices of North American supplies. Expansion was proposed with little attention to the costs falling upon the Exchequer. The government planned, and was prepared to pay for, an increase in net output over a five-year period from 1947 of 20 per cent. Although the target was attained before 1952, expansion did not precisely follow the course predicted. The output of milk and pig meat increased by more than 20 per cent, that of beef, mutton and cereals by less, while potatoes and beet sugar equalled the levels set for them. These disparities were already beginning to cause the Ministry some embarrassment by 1949, but the outbreak of the Korean War deferred any serious attempt to modify the pattern of development. At the end of the first five-year period the government set a new target for expansion, to 160 per cent of average pre-war production, but with emphasis upon cereals and beef and mutton. Nevertheless it was already clear that this plan was succeeding less well than expected, when the Minister of Agriculture decided that the era of production at any cost should be terminated in favour of a more loosely articulated system of centralised management.

The 1947 Act was not concerned solely with prices and production. Part II made far-reaching proposals for structural reform in order to increase efficiency. Planners were much interested in productivity, and the elaborate system of grants-in-aid to encourage farmers to amend or reorder agricultural and managerial techniques so as to make best use of their land, capital equipment or market opportunities was devised for this purpose. To be precise, many of the promotional subsidies on offer after 1947 were continued or modified from pre-war and wartime measures of State aid. The Ministry and even the farmers' principal spokesmen were no less certain in 1947 than in 1940 that a stick was as necessary as a carrot in driving the donkey. Thus in Part II of the Act an institution intended to persuade but capable of coercion, the County Agricultural Committees, was established on a new footing. These committees closely resembled the emergency War Agricultural Committees, and possessed the power to discipline both landowners and landholders for failure to maintain satisfactory standards of estate management or husbandry. The power stopped short of confiscation, but the committees were allowed to evict bad tenants and to impose practices of good husbandry upon owners and owner-occupiers. Extreme penalties were seldom invoked, but the committees did often intervene, during and to a lesser extent after the war, to bring derelict land, unregarded isolated plots or parts of holdings into full and profitable use. Under the War Agricultural Committees 10,000 cases of dispossession were authorised between 1940 and 1947, but few were contentious. Only about 1,400 'real' tenancies were terminated, sometimes because the farmers were obdurate against voluntary compliance but mostly

17

because they were too old, too feeble or too hopelessly disorganised to respond to suggested improvements.

Such wartime powers seem to represent ideas of coercive efficiency outside the tradition of freedom under the law. Yet most were retained after 1947, at least on paper. The acceptance of compulsion by the various landed interest groups reflects the corporative spirit of the day but was more probably regarded as a *quid pro quo* of the subsidies and producer protection provided in the Act. The old committees and the new were dominated by farmers, and their regulatory powers were seldom exercised without protracted discussion and compromise. For some agriculturists the advisory, exhortatory and coercive powers of the committees merely extended the ancient, but attenuated, privileges of the greater landowners to discipline their tenantry and at the same time made them more widely acceptable because of greater public accountability. Furthermore much of the County Committees' work was not punitive or even controversial. In the ten years of their operation the greatest volume of work was not interventionist but classificatory. Advisory work, including often the loan of equipment, had always been important, but the production drive initiated in 1947 included an extensive survey of British farming as it was, together with its potential for development. Much of this survey and classification fell upon the committees, which adopted the wartime grading system for each farm, A to C, assigned after a detailed exploration of the land, methods of cultivation, machinery, labour and output. The committees relied much upon the officials of the National Agricultural Advisory Service to prepare the reports, but if the outcome of any survey was the need to instruct or reprove the farmer or his landlord the duty of intervention fell upon the committee in whose district the holding was situated. The implications of such authority disturbed lawyers and politicians more than they apparently irritated most landholders. But the tendency to impose uniformity upon the whole of a region's agriculture, the too close association of advising and sanctions and the rather unclear status of the committees' judicial functions were controversial from the beginning.

Although the committees survived for ten years the trend of

their activities gradually declined from year to year. In a brief surge of intervention in 1952, at the height of the Korean War, 1,000 supervisions and 113 dispossessions caused some adverse comment, but Dugdale's enthusiasm soon waned. By 1957 the committees were interfering very little in matters related to good husbandry. Their work, however, was distasteful to Heathcote Amory, and he repealed Part II of the 1947 Act as soon as he was able, even though the NFU opposed the move, apparently for fear that the whole edifice of subsidisation was at risk of demolition.

Abolition of the County Agricultural Committees did not indicate that the government had lost interest in encouraging productivity, but the free-market beliefs particularly of Heathcote Amory conflicted with most of the corporative ideals enshrined in Tom William's policies. Thus the second stage in post-war agricultural planning was marked by relaxation of controls and, so far as was possible, by the substitution of cost-effectiveness for maximum production as a guide of policy. The second stage, which lasted from about 1954 to the early 1960's, was not uniform, but its achievements — derationing, the evolution of deficiency payments to maintain farmers' incomes in years of growing international surpluses, a general flight from bureaucratic interference in agriculture and, in due course, a shift in emphasis from price supports to production grants — were all pointing in the same direction.

The background to this change of course by government was the recovery and further expansion of production in all the traditional agricultural surplus areas. By the mid-1950's world-wide glut seemed to be replacing the frequent shortages in traded agricultural commodities that had clouded the immediate post-war years. Domestic output was buoyant, perhaps too much so in some products such as milk and eggs, and the anxieties over the dollar gap had receded after 1952. There was a protracted academic debate among economists about the merits of subsidising agriculture in order to achieve import savings when the prices of foreign supplies were favourable. The government pledged itself not to abandon the subsidies which guaranteed prices, but the easing of constraints upon UK food supplies gave the Minister much more room to manoeuvre than had been possible before 1953. It is, however, fair to point out that the great improvement in the terms of trade for manufacturing countries was not adequately predicted. Changes of government policy were therefore rather circumspect until the 1957 Agriculture Act, but nevertheless they still attracted opposition from some economists and the majority of interest groups.

Derationing was obviously inevitable, since it was believed to be unpopular with consumers, but it was not effected until the government was certain of adequate domestic supplies, especially of animal products, to ensure steady consumption without resort to a major increase in imports. This point was reached in 1953-54, at which time all food rationing was abolished. Decontrol, however, was a fairly complicated procedure, Since the government had allocated the enumerated agricultural commodities it had purchased to wholesalers and processors through a fairly elaborate mechanism of controls, freeing the markets meant a widespread reconstruction of the system of distribution. Some price controls, notably for milk and bread, were retained, but for the most part actual market prices were allowed to determine the prices paid by consumers. Dealers in agricultural commodities were free to buy and sell with few restrictions; traditional marketing revived, and Marketing Boards, in suspense since the war, were rehabilitated. Foreign trade, particularly imports, began to increase. Something like the commercial conditions of the 1930's reappeared, but the government, which saw certain advantages in the return of 'cheap food' as an issue of policy, was determined to protect farmers' prices. Hence the system of deficiency payments for those commodities not still subject to an administrative monopsony such as milk. The idea was to use the annual review, or, if necessary, extraordinary reviews, to fix the price standard for each product year by year. This price would be guaranteed, and any deficiency between the standard and actual market price would be compensated by the government. In the case of some commodities market prices were capable of manipulation by quasi-public agencies, but for cereals and fatstock, among many lesser products, the power to control prices was negligible. Deficiency payments suffered from the same drawback as the system of direct purchasing with guaranteed prices, since they could render the government liable to an open-ended commitment. With both domestic and world supplies improving and international prices tending to fall, the gap between market prices and 'remunerative' prices widened in the middle and later 1950's for several key commodities. The answer was to introduce a system of 'standard quantities' to set beside the 'standard prices' in the schedule of guarantees. This, however, was not an easy transition to make. The government's first response in 1953-55 was to cut guaranteed prices for commodities in surplus, especially milk and pig meat. The result was uproar among farmers. This led to a measure of appeasement, the Agricultural Act of 1957, which bound the government not to make reductions in guaranteed prices by more than 2½ per cent in any one year, after allowing in full for any change in costs. Each commodity was similarly protected, but the margins of reduction were adapted to meet the needs of particular products. In return the National Farmers' Union gave up its privilege of demanding special reviews to adjust prices in emergencies and the new arrangements proposed in the Act severely restricted the frequency of extraordinary reviews. More significantly, the Act tried to shift emphasis from straightforward price guarantees towards improvement grants. £50 million was set aside for this purpose to supplement the sums already marked for capital improvements in the current year. The Act seemed less significant at the time than it turned out to be, since the trend of policy after 1957 was to curb spending on transfer payments and to enlarge that on improvement grants. The compromise that had satisfied the union when the Act was passed proved hollow, and the annual reviews of 1958 and 1960, especially, were bitterly contested. The measure of this dissatisfaction is evident from the pricing policies of the next four years, for additions to the guarantees announced by the Ministry fell short of cost increases by over £85 million, and only in the election year of 1959 was the government willing to relax its stringent search for economies. But the inference that farmers would benefit directly from greater efficiency, not least by making better use of improvement grants, posed another problem, for the pressures upon government spending after 1953 were largely the result of rising world output. Spending, whether on guarantees or grants, seemed inexorably to encourage production at home as well.

The Ministry was unable or unwilling to force down the level of subsidies to match the increasingly stringent demands of the Treasury. After 1960 the NFU mended its fences with the government, and the Minister attempted new ways to cut the overall cost of subsidisation by fixing import quotas for certain commodities in surplus. At the same time the 'standard quantity' for domestic produce, especially when protected from overseas competition, was employed more efficiently. From 1963 several products were so regulated. Any surplus above the quantity budgeted by the Minister was unsubsidised and had to find its own price. The idea was that excess production would gradually be liquidated because it was unremunerative, but the plan overlooked the momentum of growth. Nevertheless the Ministry, after ten years of trial and error, had at last found an instrument with which to close the 'open end' of price subsidisation without impairing agricultural prosperity significantly or undermining the regime of 'cheap food'.

The third stage of agricultural policy in a sense begins with the introduction of import quotas in 1962, but there is no clear evidence of any sharp break in trend. The new government in 1964 promised a fresh approach to virtually every aspect of the economy, including agriculture, but apart from a convoluted land policy the results were not especially distinguished. The

Agricultural subsidies (£ million)

Year	Gross output	Price guarantees	Grants and subsidies
1958–59	1,452·2	181·3	83·8
1959–60	1,468·6	154·7	95·1
1960–61	1,497·6	151·2	104·5
1961–62	1,606·6	225·5	107·5
1962–63	1,639·5	190·1	109·4
1963–64	1,662·0	186·8	102·8
1971–72	2,370	144·3	182·7

previous administration, less enthusiastic for liberalisation than in the mid-1950's, had initiated several new lines of policy upon which Fred Peart could build. Essentially the modified scheme of deficiency payments and improvement grants administered by Christopher Soames at the end of the Macmillan era was continued throughout the 1960's. Until the major sterling crisis in 1967 the Labour government was rather more interested in structural reform. Thus the lack of farmers' co-operation was discerned as a deficiency to be remedied by government assistance. The 1967 Agriculture Act set aside £40 million over five years to further the cause, and a Council for Agricultural and Horticultural Co-operation was instituted to administer the grants. At the same time the difficulties of small farmers were widely publicised. Amalgamation was the solution preferred by most agricultural planners. Thus grants were made available from 1967 to encourage private consolidation of holdings, but this was felt to be insufficient. Continental experience suggested that State intervention might be necessary to achieve effective rationalisation. Government hankering after land nationalisation was hardly translated into policies in the 1960's but it reinforced the belief in 'purposive' intervention. The Minister proposed to encourage voluntary sales of farm land to the State, as well as to private individuals, in order to bring about amalgamation, and offered generous payments to occupants of uncommercial holdings to speed up the process of retirement and redeployment. A good example of the new enthusiasm for planning was the proposal for Rural Development Boards in the 1967 Act, which would have had quite wide powers to reconstruct the agricultural organisation of hill-farming districts But only the Pennine RDB was founded, and it had a short life because it proved distinctly unpopular among farmers. Thirdly, the Minister was concerned to complete the reform of agricultural marketing. The Meat and Livestock Commission, which was created under the 1967 Act, was somewhat different both from the existing Marketing Boards and from other public monopolies like the British Sugar Corporation, but, given the much more loosely constructed system of meat trading, the Commission was intended to perform essentially the same function.

Nineteen-sixty-seven also marked a return to 'import saving' as a major object of agricultural policy. Acute economic difficulties encouraged the belief that agriculture could ease balance of payments deficits, but the decision in 1966 again to pursue application to join the Common Market prompted the Ministry to investigate the means of correlating British and European agricultural policies. This clearly implied a reduction of UK dependence upon imported foodstuffs. It led to a relaxation of restrictions through the application of standard quantities; imports were regulated by market-sharing agreements with various governments; and more grants directed at raising productivity were authorised. The consequence was that more of the costs of supporting agriculture were transferred from the Treasury and taxpayer to the consumer than would have been politically feasible in the 1950's. In effect retail food prices rose somewhat faster than domestic production, although greater self-sufficiency was achieved in the ten years after 1965. The new course was not particularly popular, but the burden upon consumers was not substantial, since food prices rose by 44 per cent in 1965-73 whereas total personal income increased by 70 per cent. Even so, many of the government's supporters at the end of the 1960's objected that shifting the burden to the consumer was detrimental to the economy as a whole. Nor was international opinion especially favourable, since the government began to move towards greater protectionism when the General Agreement on Tariffs and Trade (GATT) was liberalising the system of international trade.

From the point of view of the Treasury, however, the financial adjustments were successful, whatever the wider consequences of the import-saving policy. Agricultural subsidies cost £206 million in 1955-56, £265 million in 1964-65 and £273 million in 1970-71. Since farmers were not signally starved of income in the late 1960's, it is evident that consumers had been called up into the front line to cover the retreat of the Exchequer. Expectations of joining the Common Market rather clouded the issue of reduced subsidisation among agricultural interest groups, which regarded the prospect with some apprehension but were prepared to accept the change from price support to production grant in the late 1950's and from deficiency payments to levies and rebates in the 1970's. The complexity of British participation in the CAP, however, requires separate treatment.

The financial support of prices or plans for the structural reform of agriculture were but part of the thesaurus of policies for intervention during and after the second world war. Wage regulation had been introduced before the war but was made more effective and wider-ranging after 1940. During the same period control over the working conditions of workers on the land was increased, especially with regard to safety. By the late 1960's farms were subject to most of the same regulations relating to employees' welfare at work as any other establishment. The statutory requirements for protective devices have become extensive in the past twenty-five years. Yet farms are still quite dangerous places at which to work, chiefly because enforcement of the safety provisions has been difficult. Day-to-day supervision of practices by farmers and workers is impossible. The result of surveys into farm accidents suggests that most have been caused by lapses of concentration or through reluctance to follow recommended procedures. In other words, intervention by government has not failed directly to improve conditions of work; the failure has been of exhortation or explanation. It is a mark of the weakness of the trade unions in agriculture that the work force has not been effectively persuaded to insist upon the application of safety regulations and to make use of their provisions. Farm accidents reported to the authorities reached a peak in the early 1960's. The effort put into propaganda then had some effect, for by 1970 the level of accidents had declined by 15-20 per cent, but accidents caused by machinery, despite improved design, remained numerous throughout the 1970's, although there were fewer severe cases by 1975 than in 1968.

Looking back over the past forty years, it is clear that some degree of intervention, price support and exhortation has been accepted by all parties as a necessary fact of economic and political life. The contrast with the 1920's is striking, but recollection of retreat from subsidisation after the first world war was sufficient to maintain the political consensus, especially in the 1950's, for not even Heathcote Amory abandoned the premise of support in some kind. The enthusiasm of most farmers' interest groups for subsidies may

have belied their political Conservatism but doubtless held the
Tory Party steady. Parliamentary opposition was erratic and
usually ineffectual. Both Labour members, disconcerted by the
spectacle of 'feather-bedded' farmers, and Conservatives,
rather more anxious about the bureaucracy of planning or the
emergence of food surpluses, were to be found sniping at
Ministers in every Parliament between 1945 and 1974, but,
until the Common Agricultural Policy focused attention on the
less palatable aspects of agricultural support, dissentient
voices were drowned in the persistent murmur of acquiescence.
In the event the Conservative Party drifted further away from
the consensus politics of the late 1950's when, under Edward
Heath, it began the process of redefining its ideals and came
out with the blueprint for 'Selsdon man' as the *beau ideal* of
modern Toryism in the late 1960's. But the result, in the
government of 1970-74, did not fulfil all the expectations of
1969, not least because embracing the Common Market with
unprecedented eagerness laid the government open to an
even more numbing barrage of interventionist regulations.

Outside Parliament the attack on bureaucratic collectivism
concentrated little fire upon agriculture. Journalists such as
Colm Brogan and academics like Hayek and Jewkes who
disparaged socialist planning with enthusiasm had better
things to do than to take apart the preconceptions of government agricultural policy. Within the food industries the only
consistent opponents of agricultural subsidisation throughout
the 1940's and 1950's were the Farmers and Smallholders
Association and the Cheap Food League, neither of which
carried any weight in the formulation of policy. Individual
agriculturists, however, as the frequent criticism of marketing
schemes indicates, were often less complacent about intervention than their official spokesmen.

Farmers reject the notion that their industry has been
'feather-bedded' at the expense of other sections of the
economy since the war. Certainly the Treasury has not been
an endless cornucopia of transfer payments to enrich the
already well endowed in the countryside. The vigour with
which many annual reviews were contested, and the
sometimes abrupt changes of direction in support policies,
suggest that if the well did not run dry the water pumped out

was not always of the sweetest. Nevertheless susidisation did raise farm incomes substantially and protected agriculture from the effects of broad fluctuations in the outside world.

3 · Agriculture and the Common Market

The most important turning point in agricultural policy occurred when the United Kingdom joined the European Economic Community. But the date of admission, 1 January 1973, was not in itself a major event. Plans for entry had been laid for some time in order to make the transition of policy and agricultural practice as fluent as possible, and even after 1973 there was a lengthy term of adjustment before Britain, the Republic of Ireland and Denmark were fully assimilated into the system of intervention prescribed in the Treaty of Rome. The prospects and consequences of membership influenced British agricultural planning for almost two decades. The Common Agricultural Policy had developed along a course similar to that followed in Britain, but the premises upon which agricultural support were established owed nothing to the ties of cheap food. Amendments to British policy were therefore inevitable, since the Common Agricultural Policy could not diplomatically be altered to satisfy specific British needs. The protracted period of adjustment indicates just how difficult and sensitive the changes were, since no British government in the ten years after 1961 was able to introduce radical new policies in preparation for admission, and the abortive negotiations of that decade tended to set back internal progress towards 'harmonisation' because the outcome was so uncertain.

The essential features of the Common Agricultural Policy were laid down in Article 39 of the Treaty of Rome. As stated the objectives differ hardly at all from the intentions enshrined in the 1947 Agriculture Act:

(a) to increase agricultural productivity through technical progress and by ensuring the rational development of production and the optimum use of the factors of production, especially labour;

(b) to ensure a fair standard of living for the agricultural community, especially to increase farm incomes;
(c) to stabilise markets;
(d) to secure regular supplies;
(e) to maintain supplies to consumers at reasonable prices.

As in Britain there was much uncertainty about the compati-
bility of different objects of policy. The hopes contained in a
diplomatic construct, the Treaty of Rome, had to be translated
into reality by hard bargaining. The result of such compro-
mises effectively rearranged the priorities, sometimes in the
teeth of logical necessity. Each member State had a heritage of
agricultural policy and resources of self-regard that had to be
accommodated in the common interest. But quite apart from
the fact that in the 1950's shortage of foreign exchange and
the fear of dearth influenced decision-making in all the countries of western Europe, the tradition of agricultural policy on
the Continent had always concentrated upon protecting and
supporting farmers (sc. peasants) if necessary at the expense
of urban and industrial consumers. Two consequences followed
from this emphasis in policy-making: first, that full producer
protection was an agreed principle and, secondly, that since
past policies had tended to bolster up small-scale, fragmented
peasant regimes of cultivation, there was a general will after
the war to promote land reforms for the sake of efficiency. To
enhance the position of the producer against that of the consumer was not expressed in the treaty but it was implicit in the
agreements made at the time. The last provision, especially the
adjective 'reasonable', was too vague to act as a counterpoise
to the others, not least because most European consumers had
long been used to prices strongly affected by tariffs against
foreign competition. On the other hand, although the
negotiators were aware that international conditions had
changed with the return of surpluses in the mid-1950's, the
persistence of plenty during the early years of the Common
Agricultural Policy meant that the costs of maintaining
improved productivity, farm incomes and stable markets were
more expensive than predicted. It is an interesting question
whether Article 39 would have been different or differently
interpreted had it been framed a few years later. For several
countries with large agricultural sectors the fact of world

surpluses was more menacing than the period of shortages.

The price system of the Common Agricultural Policy is relatively straightforward in design, although it often becomes convoluted in practice. For each commodity a target price is assigned. Imports are permitted only if it is believed that the price fixed for domestic producers will not be jeopardised, which means that in most years imports of temperate agricultural produce are discouraged. In the case of surpluses, which if placed on the market would depress prices, various official agencies are required to buy the stocks at what is called the intervention price, i.e. at slightly below the target price, and to hold the commodities in store. Intervention stocks may be kept until market prices have risen and then sold, thus acting as a stabilising influence upon trade, or in some instances they may be exported to relieve the accumulation of permanent surpluses.

The cost of this operation, intended originally to be used only in extraordinary circumstances, is provided from a fund administered by FEOGA (European Agricultural Guarantee and Guidance Fund), which receives the levies imposed on agricultural imports. Since it was not expected that intervention would be necessary in every year, the income from import levies, accumulated through time, was expected to be sufficient of finance the scheme. But the self-financing regime of FEOGA faltered in the late 1960's when the emergence of permanent food surpluses raised the cost of guarantees for both intervention and export subsidies. Since the UK became a member of the EEC the treasuries of the constituent States have been compelled to augment the fund in every year.

For the policy to be a success the choice of each year's target price has been vitally important. The pressure of farmers' lobbies throughout the Community and the reluctance of governments with large peasant constituencies to face the political consequences of too low prices reinforced the intention of the Commission to raise average farm incomes, with the result that for most commodities and in most years the target prices were set too high. The outcome was rapidly increasing production. Since the 1960's technical advances were tending to enlarge productivity everywhere in the developed world, but the restraints upon excess production generally caused by the downward adjustment of prices were ineffective in the Common Market. At almost every turn opportunities to alter internal prices were resisted by governments. Thus when the original notion that uniform agricultural prices were to be maintained by fixed exchange rates was undermined by fluctuations in the values of different currencies, adjustments to the system of units of account used in making payments by the Commission were inadequate, ineffective or delayed. The first case, in 1969, when the Deutschemark was revalued and the French franc devalued, was inauspicious, for the Germans, who should have allowed their domestic agricultural prices to decline, refused to do so, especially since the French devaluation had the effect of raising agricultural prices in France. Thus, instead of an open trade in farm produce, the traffic in commodities between Germany and her partners was subjected to fiscal adjustments, additional levies on German imports and subsidies on her exports. The problem recurred in the 1970's when, in a period of floating exchange rates, the Commission devised a new method of calculating payments within the CAP, the so-called 'green' currencies, which were adjusted upward or downward not necessarily according to the oscillations of real exchange rates but in order to satisfy the political aspirations of member governments anent their agricultural sectors. Even the evolution of a common standard of currency within the European Monetary System did not relieve the problems of CAP finances, partly because not all currencies have been integrated in the 'Snake', and partly because the habit among governments of protecting their agriculturists against the movement of the exchanges has become too deeply ingrained.

In this way the simple dispositions of the Treaty of Rome not only became complex but also disquietingly expensive. Subsidies in order to guarantee prices became very burdensome upon the Commission's annual budgets. In 1962-63 guarantees cost 28·7 million units of account; by 1968-69 this had already risen to 1,642·9 million. An attempt to rein in expenditure in 1970 was only briefly successful. In 1974, when world prices were notably higher than in the late 1960's, subsidies amounted only to 1,700 million units of account. Thereafter, however, the rate of increase, even allowing for the

31

three new members, was acute: in 1978 2,697 million units and 3,841 million in 1982. By the early 1980's spending upon guarantees to the diary sector, when there was a large surplus of all dairy produce, consumed about 75 per cent of the total CAP budget. It is almost axiomatic that the sectors with the largest surpluses in store should be the most heavily subsidised.

Favourable prices and substantial increments of productivity have resulted in self-sufficiency in virtually all temperate agricultural commodities. By 1970, just before the Community was enlarged, there were regular surpluses, not always exportable, in wheat, barley, sugar and dairy produce and deficiencies only in maize, beef and veal and lamb. The shortages of 1972, which threatened to overturn the settled pattern of trading surpluses in foods, braced EEC determination to maintain autarky and caused the Commission to offer greater subsidies for maize and oil plants, in the latter case because it was feared that the American monopoly of soya production might affect European access to apparently scarce supplies.

One great problem of the CAP is that actual or potential demand is not closely related to price. Western Europe could certainly consume the intervention stocks of butter, beef and pig meat if prices were adjusted to the state of the market. In the case of surpluses for which demand is relatively inelastic, such as sugar and cereals, output would obviously be adjusted to meet demand, if the target prices were reduced. Such a course of action is difficult, although, in instances of blatant excess, amendments have been forced through the committee of Ministers of Agriculture. Ironically one such adjustment, an attempt to give greater financial support to arable production at the expense of dairying in the early 1970's, caused an increase of output in both.

What is lacking in the CAP is an effective check upon quantities in relation to price guarantees. The British government discovered at the end of the 1950's that the domestic system of deficiency payments could be made accountable to the Exchequer only if it was linked to limits upon production known as 'standard quantities'. Producer protection works in the long term if output can be restrained in order to stabilise market prices. This can be achieved in several different ways, none of which has been coherently attempted under the CAP. Making payments to farmers in terms of actual output at some date in the past has been imposed from time to time, particularly in the dairy sector, but it has not produced any long-term stabilisation of production and it has seldom been applied for more than short periods. The pressure of both governments and interest groups against severe curtailment of agricultural production has been irresistible because prices have been viewed in relation to the plan for raising and maintaining farm incomes. The CAP was a scheme to protect the mass of poorer peasant farmers whose holdings were not commercially viable. It has resulted in the well-found doing even better. This has been a common problem of all agricultural support schemes since the 1930's, but in the Common Market a specific defect has been compounded into a general failing, because the Commission has few powers of coercion or effective regulation with which to redress the internal balance.

However, the CAP was formulated with some of these problems in mind. Expert opinion tended to hold that structural reform would resolve many of the discrepancies caused by the coexistence of large and small holdings. Since price guarantees were intended as a measure to assist the less successful among producers, structural reforms would eventually make the props unnecessary or at least supererogatory because uneconomic holdings would have been eliminated or improved. The prognosis was improbable and was, in any event, obscured by the rather erratic progress of rationalisation. Policies directed to amalgamation, realignment of fields and farm layouts, investment in new buildings, drainage, reclamation and afforestation (of very low quality land) were numerous and often successful, although many were devised and administered by member governments, not by the Commission.

The most important of these improvements has been the campaign to consolidate farms and to eradicate economically unimprovable peasant holdings. The methods have been different in each country, but the results have been similar everywhere. The number of agricultural holdings has diminished steadily since the second world war throughout the original Six. In 1958 there were more than 6·6 million holdings of more than one hectare in the Six. In Germany, Belgium and the Netherlands numbers halved in the following twenty years, and within the original member States there were only about 4·6 million by 1980, of which about half were classified as full-time, against 40 per cent at the beginning of the EEC's existence. These figures compare well with the data of decline in the United Kingdom, but since the average size of holdings had been so much less on the Continent there is still a substantial difference between Britain and the other eight member States. On the other hand, in countries traditionally as firmly wedded to subsistence peasantry as were Germany and France the reform of uneconomic holdings and the capture of the centre ground in agricultural politics by farmers with substantial holdings have been remarkable developments of the past twenty years.

In other parts of the Common Market the solution to the problem of *morcellement* has been to encourage part-time farming. In parts of southern Germany, for example, the apparent failure of amalgamation is to be explained in precisely these terms. The political outcome of both trends, however, has not been a significant relaxation of governments' protectiveness towards their agricultural sectors, since in France farmers' lobbying has become even more intensive and well organised and in Germany and Belgium the part-time occupation of the land has not reduced the need of peasants to make a profit from their agriculture. Indeed, because so many of the smaller farmers on good soils have done very well out of the CAP, particularly in Germany and the Low Countries, demands to maintain the new peasant affluence have become even more strident.

Structural reform has not gone as far as is possible. In Italy and Ireland progress was slow before the late 1970's. EEC price support policies may indeed, have worked actively against consolidation in the peripheral areas. Subsidising both Mediterranean agriculture and marginal pastoral agriculture was socially necessary because of the heritage of poverty among peasants in such districts but it tended both to exacerbate budgetary problems and to create tensions between member States, and even among farmers within particular countries.

The EEC left much of the planning for structural reform to the States themselves, but by the mid-1960's this was thought to be insufficient because it imposed financial obligations upon the Commission, particularly in areas slow to rationalise farm structures, without giving Brussels adequate discretion in allocating agricultural funds. The Commission therefore set up an inquiry which in 1967 produced a plan, largely the work of Sicco Mansholt, the commissioner responsible for agriculture, to standardise and co-ordinate the consolidation of farms, the realignment of plots, the shake-out of farmers and farm workers who were too old or underemployed, and, more tentatively, to encourage changes in land use. Modernisation of agricultural practices, schemes of training and retraining and the provision of a common advisory service followed directly from the Mansholt report. The results in the core regions of temperate Europe were satisfactory, but intervention in the peripheral regions of the south and pastoral west was less striking. The Mansholt plan has added a new dimension to the CAP. It has contributed something to the support of structural adjustment in Britain since 1973. Yet it was largely overtaken by events. The assimilation of the three new members in the 1970's and the subsequent over-extension of the budgetary commitments of the CAP diminished the force of the plan, even though new directives dealing with structural problems were regularly issued during the 1970's.

When the United Kingdom joined the EEC the wide difference between British agricultural policy and the CAP were recognised in the arrangements made to integrate the new members with the old during a five-year transitional period. There was little doubt in official circles in Britain after the early 1960's that the United Kingdom would have to adapt to existing policies derived from the Treaty of Rome, and some movement towards the EEC pricing system had been made unilaterally before the third phase of negotiation began after 1970. The agreement which became operative in 1973 prescribed that UK food prices should gradually be brought into line with those prevailing in the Six. Free trade in agricultural produce would be modified by the application of transitional compensatory amounts, under which imports from the EEC into Britain would receive a subsidy equal to the current difference in prices. After completion of the transitional period in January 1978 the UK would become an equal member of the Community. As it turned out, the much higher rate of inflation in Britain, by comparison with the remainder of the EEC, distorted the operation of these provisions, and in certain commodities, notably butter, subsidised prices for the consumer continued to be conceded for fear that if British prices were forced upwards to the level prevailing on the Continent demand would collapse. In other respects internal free trade was compromised by special conditions attached to particular commodities, including some imports from outside the EEC, above all to butter and lamb from New Zealand. British reluctance to accept the full implications of the Common Market in agricultural products, even after 1978, in order to protect domestic consumers and Commonwealth suppliers, provided ammunition for sniping among member States but simply exemplified the widespread dilemma between national and Community interests throughout the Nine.

The British had to accept other equally unpalatable changes. The superficial similarity of political conditions in which every European country had since the war managed its agricultural policy in a spirit of compromise with its most powerful agrarian interest groups disguised conflicting traditions. The long-standing British concern with cheap food and the openness of markets did not square with the Continental preference for tariffs and 'producer-determined' prices. The United Kingdom had been surprisingly effective in balancing the interests of domestic agriculture and of oversea suppliers, of producers and consumers, in periods of plenty as in scarcity. In the early 1960's the British were believed to enjoy the cheapest and the best food in Europe, in terms of range and variety. This had been achieved at the same time as our proportions of self-sufficiency had been improved. The filaments of international trade in foodstuffs had ramified into most nations of the Commonwealth capable of producing food surpluses and into many others, rich and poor, from the United States to Poland or Uruguay. The United Kingdom was the largest open market for temperate foodstuffs in the world and hence an object of special interest to the Six as much as to Argentina, New Zealand and Canada. The implication of British accession was that sooner or later external suppliers of food would be excluded from the British market in the interests of the EEC. Protecting the interests of New Zealand and of former British sugar islands was as far as the United Kingdom could go in minimising the shock to world trade of the virtual closure of British markets. At the time of accession temporary shortages and the apparently bleak prospects for agricultural production in an overpopulated world lessened the impact of the change but the reappearance of plenty in the late 1970's has revived the issue, not least because the discrepancy between EEC and world food prices has again become too obvious to be ignored.

Another problem for the British has been to align their highly capitalised and commercialised agricultural structure to the different agrarian regimes of the continent. Much ink was spent in rather scornful comparisons between British farmers and continental peasants. Most of the shafts missed the target, because, in terms of production, and in many instances of productivity, EEC 'peasants' could often equal if not outperform the capital-intensive farmers of Britain. Efficiency in land use is not necessarily a function of size or capital intensity. A peasant with a share in a co-operative for marketing his produce and with access to cheap or subsidised supplies of credit, with favourable tax provisions and in expectation of at least stable prices, was certainly not among that marginal or residual social class surviving only because of its political influence which played so large a part in British interpretations of the EEC scene. Moreover the convergence of policies to promote consolidation did not result in an identical tendency towards capital intensivity: the British commitment to expensive 'high farming' was not necessarily imitated on the Continent, even by progressive agriculturists.

The United Kingdom agricultural sector, already thoroughly embrued with a commercial tincture, stood to gain substantially from the operation of the CAP, since in 1973 British farmers were already obtaining yields in most commodities at or near the top of the range of productivity in the world.

They had been used for generations to compete with imports, and nothing in the planned system of guaranteed payments appeared to conflict with their established interests. Their marketing system seemed to be as effective as anything in the Six. Costs, though high, were believed to be manageable, since they were set off against burgeoning output. Moreover, since internal subsidies to help sections of the industry to maintain or extend markets were illicit under CAP rules, most British farmers were satisfied that they could hold their position and would probably thrive in the EEC. Some were obviously more vulnerable than others. Horticulture and perhaps pig farming were uncertainly placed, and there were real doubts about the long-run prosperity of dairying, given the surpluses which already existed within the Six. Gloomy prophecies that mainstream activities such as cereal growing and cattle rearing might suffer and that Britain, more generally, might become as peripheral in west European agriculture as the Western Isles in relation to mainland Britain were founded upon a misreading of the auguries. With modern arable technology the marginal quality of much British arable land does not signify. The extent to which France in particular can concentrate production of common tillage crops in areas where soil and climate are most favourable to their growth will always be limited by the ability of other regions to make a technologically effective response and by the political balancing that takes place every year at meetings of member Ministers of Agriculture. If the EEC were to become a unitary State the situation might well be different. Otherwise British arable farmers can expect to do as well economically as their Continental counterparts.

Southern and Midland England certainly, and probably north-eastern England and eastern Scotland also, are potentially as much as actually as good arable terrain as almost any part of the EEC. Equally most of the naturally good grassland of Britain is not inferior to permanent pasture on the Continent. In the 1970's the changes that occurred in land use in Britain did not lead to a sectional decline in agriculture. Arable farming has proved to be more remunerative than pastoral husbandry, except dairying, but farmers have been sufficiently adaptable to expand one branch of production at the expense, but not to the detriment, of another. In the future this skewing of land use in favour of tillage may not persist. Britain is sufficiently well endowed with productive soils to allow subsequent generations to modify their enterprises successfully. In other words the grounds for pessimism so far as international comparisons are concerned were untenable in the late 1960's and have not become more convincing since British accession. What stands out from inspection of the evidence is that trends which set in after the war in Britain have been reinforced, not overturned, by application of the Common Agricultural Policy.

Many of the problems facing British agriculturists and successive Ministers since 1973 have been tactical rather than strategic. The recurrent disputes over allegedly hidden subsidies, or over subsidies which, though not strictly illegal, have been regarded as improper by competitors, provide much insight into the varieties of misunderstanding. Because so much depends upon negotiation in EEC affairs, claims and counter-claims have become a tedious fact of life. Britain has been in an especially vulnerable position. As the chief region of deficiency in domestic food production the UK has been an object of keen interest to the French, the Irish, the Dutch and the Danes in particular. Allegations of dumping, of special aids being offered to penetrate the British market, and, more directly, of hidden subsidies by member governments and not authorised by the Commission, have been commonplace since the mid-1970's, though they have not all been proved. However, since the implications of a completely free internal trade are often too painful for producers or their governments to contemplate, means of subverting harmful developments in commercial exchanges are constantly being devised to frustrate competitors and even to outwit the Commission and the European Court. Thus, when the French threatened to seize a large share of the British trade in poultry meat at the end of the 1970's, protestations of unfair assistance were rife and the British government, not being able to establish proof, chose instead to impose a ban on French poultry imports on the grounds that there was a risk of contagion by Newcastle's disease, eradicated from Britain but still endemic in France. Another example of international rivalry in the Community is the British objection to Dutch fuel subsidies for glasshouse growers of fruit and vegetables, which were blamed for the poor competitive position of British horticulturists. Even when governments have not been averse from reducing or abolishing financial inducements, agricultural interest groups have sometimes been able to prevent action at least until such time as the European Court has passed judgement. Holding out after the Court's injunction has been made is much more difficult but not in fact impossible.

Details such as these irritate governments and their public alike. They certainly exemplify the lack of community spirit that envelops the bargaining process at all levels. They overlie a fundamental deformity of structure which is the cause of most of the quarrelsomeness. The premise upon which the system of inter-State payments for agriculture was founded was not intended to support conditions of continuous surplus and divergent international prices. At the outset of its membership the United Kingdom was required to make a net contribution to the EEC in the form of agricultural levies upon its imports of £70 million, despite the transitional arrangements. The outflow of British revenues to the EEC was set to rise steeply, for even in 1973 the estimate by the Treasury assumed a net contribution by 1980 of £380 million. In the event the figures turned out to be significantly larger, for by the last date the UK was paying a contribution of more than £800 million.

Hence the complaints of unfairness and the demand for renegotiation by the Labour government in 1974-75. Even after 'renegotiation' there was continuous pressure by both Labour and Conservative governments to reduce the outflow and claim rebates. The special pleading has produced results. It was recently asserted that about 60 per cent of British payments in agricultural levies had been returned. Even so, there is a crisis every year over the British rebate, with threats and counter-threats until such time as some compromise is agreed in order to ward off the ultimate disorder of insolvency in the Commission and intransigent irredentism among governments. The problem is that the whole financial constitution of the CAP has broken through the Kennelly-Heaviside layer in expenditure and can hardly be restrained without major reconstruction, even though the terms of the Treaty of Rome have become almost sacrosanct as a monument of primordial ideals.

However, the disputes and discordant opinions expressed through inter-government 'negotiations' well up from below the ministerial level. As in domestic policy-making, there is both national and international public opinion, which is often divided but tends to deplore the relative insignificance of consumer interests in shaping CAP measures. Consumer interests, so-called, are represented in Brussels as they are in national affairs by organised lobbies, but they have almost always been outmanoeuvred or outgunned by COPA, the confederation of farmers' associations. COPA indeed has acquired much the same ascendancy in lobbying the Commission, the European Parliament and the Council of Ministers as the NFU achieved at home in the heyday of domestic agricultural planning before 1970. In the 1970's British attitudes were not concentrated on a particular issue, unless it was the 'unfairness' of the terms of admission, which because ill founded elicited little sympathy on the Continent. Farmers were apprehensive about their long-run prosperity under the new regime and were not averse even from self-interested criticism of the CAP on their own account. The fact that most British agriculturists had benefited substantially, perhaps even unexpectedly, from the policy by the early 1980's diminished opposition to detailed aspects of the EEC system among farmers, but redoubled the feelings of disquiet among other groups in British society. To some extent the unpopularity of the CAP in Britain in the past few years has been conveyed also to British agriculture, as a principal beneficiary, when so many other sections of the economy have gained nothing and perhaps contributed much to the continuation and protection of the Common Agricultural Policy.

4 · The pattern of farming: crops and livestock

There are in Great Britain about 45 million acres available for agricultural use of some kind. More than a third of this area, however, has always been classified as rough grazing, incapable of producing crops and carrying a very small weight of livestock per acre. Since the war less than 30 million acres have been in regular cultivation in tillage or as permanent grass. Because the better land is found in regions where the demand for building and recreational land has been a constant force for over two centuries, the quantity of cultivable land has been diminishing ever since agricultural statistics were first collected. Between 1891-1900 and 1951-60 about 3·6 million acres were deducted from the total, although since the area described as rough grazing has substantially increased, from under 13 million acres about 1900 to over 16 million around 1960, the losses to urban and industrial development are far from clear. It seems, however, that about 50,000 acres a year in the 1930's were added to the built-up area and that this had risen to 80,000 acres in the late 1950's and 1960's. How much new land was added by reclamation is not certain, but it was insufficient, apparently, to offset the losses. Moreover, reclamation was feasible only in certain marshland or moorland districts, usually quite remote from the built-up area. Farm land seems often to have been preferred for building by planners even when poor-grade heath has been available, because the recreational or conservational value of the latter has been given a higher priority than food production. Except in remote places the scope for reclamation has tended to be restricted by public disquiet over the ecological consequences of drainage or land clearance. As a result most of the new land brought into cultivation has been in small parcels. Nineteenth-century optimism that nearly all land below the tree line was improvable, which produced both the public will for reclamation on a grand scale and much private enterprise — exemplified by the notorious Sutherland improver Patrick Sellar, who thought he could plough northern peat bogs — has not been much in evidence in the affluent mid-twentieth century. The best prospect for new accretions of good farm land is around the Wash, where reclamation has been almost continuous for centuries but is still economically worth the attempt.

The net loss of farm land has not been very significant for agricultural production, but farmers' interests have nevertheless been well represented in such causes as the campaigns against the siting of a new airport at Stansted, against the selection of a 'greenfield' site for London's third airport and against the plan to mine coal near Selby and in the Vale of Belvoir. A yardstick of more importance is the balance in the cultivated area between arable and grass. England and Wales have traditionally been divided roughly equally between land in tillage and land under permanent grass. The balance has always tilted one way or the other under the influence of prevailing market conditions, but at least a third of the available cultivated land has been in tillage and a third in permanent grass, the remainder being allocated to one mode or the other according to the ascendency of 'corn or horn'. In Scotland fluctuations have been less, since only about a third of the cultivated area has generally been in grass and the remainder has been kept in tillage whatever the state of the markets.

The acreage in arable production reached its lowest point in 1938. In that year 11·86 million acres were ploughed, by comparison with 17·4 million in permanent grass. During the war the ploughing campaign reversed these figures. In 1944 17·9 million acres were in tillage and only 10·8 million in grass. The post-war decline was not precipitate: 1950, 17·million acres; 1955, 16·6 million acres; 1965, 17·5 million acres; 1975, 16·6 million acres; 1980, 16·2 million acres. The area under the plough fell only until 1957-58, so that even in the midst of the first post-war glut in world food supplies British farmers were not compelled, as they had been in the 1920's, to abandon tillage. In the 1960's, when the tide of official opinion had set towards import-saving self-sufficiency, the acreage under crops increased by half a million, which were chiefly sown to grain. The setback from the late 1960's onwards seems to have been caused by the rapidly increasing costs in relation to income from the sale of cereals, which was only partly corrected by subsidies. The ebb and flow of profitability in wheat and barley growing has made a much more limited impact upon tillage than might have been expected, chiefly, no doubt, because the high capital cost of arable farming has deterred wholesale movements in and out of arable or pasture. The frontier or the line of demarcation between predominantly arable and predominantly pastoral modes of land use, tradi- tionally dividing east and west in Britain, was re-established in the 1940's near the position it had traced a century before and has altered little since. On the other hand the overall pattern is less clear cut than in the 1840's and 1850's. There is more arable land in the west, especially on the clay lowlands, because technical improvements have extended the potential area in tillage quite considerably. By the same token the revival of dairying in the east has caused some formerly arable ground to be kept in permanent grass. Even so, it remains true that the East Riding, Norfolk and the Lothians are essentially arable districts, Cheshire, Somerset and Ayrshire essentially pastoral.

Farmers have always known how diverse the soils and con- ditions for growth are on their own farms, but land classi- fication as a science has made great strides in Britain since the 1930's. The work of independent geographers, the Land Utilisation Survey and the contribution made by the NAAS have corroborated the accumulated experience of centuries. Analysis is now so accurate that the agricultural *response* in correcting deficiencies of fertility and water retention has become very precise. There are limits to the standardisation of soil fertility, many not affected by surface geology, but the work done since the war in improving the terrain of British agriculture must be emphasised. Farmers in the post-war period have been able to depend upon inherited residues of productivity, the accumulation of returns earned from generations of steady investment in drainage, careful tillage, fertilisation, marling, liming, etc. However, the new techno- logies of land improvement, based upon a better scientific knowledge of the soil and its substrata, have since the 1950's so raised the productivity of the soil than many of the old conservational practices of husbandry have been abandoned. Underdrainage is now a fairly exact science; top-dressing and fertilisation can be measured precisely to produce distinctive results; techniques of cultivation have been modified, not necessarily without adverse side-effects, in order to make best use both of modern machinery and modern ideas of tillage and grassland management. In some respects the heritage of the past has been embarrassing, for hedgerows, trees, shallow drains have frequently been obstacles to progress, however great their aesthetic and ecological appeal.

Surface geology may no longer be a factor limiting agricultural expansion, but it remains the case that at least three-fifths of the land surface available to farmers cannot even now be cultivated either in tillage or in an alternation of arable and pasture. The major part of Britain is still in permanent, often very poor, grass. The deciding issue seldom depends upon soil type alone. What limits the spread of the plough deep into the north and west of the island is temperature, rainfall, altitude, infestation with stones, all of which are much more difficult to amend than soil fertility or moisture levels. Each of these constraints upon productivity is accounted for in modern assessments of soil classification. Britain has a very productive agricultural sector and the climate may be better adapted for farming than in most other parts of the world. Yet in terms of land utilisation the quality of the soil is not outstandingly favourable. First-rate land occupies only about 5 per cent of Britain, or about 2·3 million acres, and good land no more than a quarter of the whole area. Forty per cent has been classified as poor land, much of it essentially unimprovable even now, except perhaps through afforestation. Some soils have certainly become impoverished through human agency in the past, especially bracken-infested moorlands, but in most instances poor land is a curse of nature. Most of the poorest land is to be found in the highland zone, where all the limiting influences upon effective agriculture are in force, and most of the better land lies in the east, especially in the south-east of the island, where tillage is practicable almost everywhere. Nevertheless there is good land in the west, above all in the broader river valleys, and poor land, often thin sand, in the east.

The inherent quality of the land does determine the pattern

of agriculture, but where climate, slope and altitude are not unfavourable it has been possible to change the prevailing regime quite successfully, as with the development of intensive cultivation in the Norfolk Breckland or the ploughing of upper slopes in the downland landscapes of England. On the other hand, no one has repeated the attempts of both medieval and early nineteenth-century farmers to till the Pennine moorlands above north-country industrial towns. It is also probable that the hard labour of farmers and farm workers between 1760 and 1850 in clearing stones, rooting out bracken and building up soil fertility in marginal districts such as south central Devon or central Aberdeenshire and the Mearns would not be attempted now had the pioneering work not already been achieved. In general the pendulum of tillage has swung as far as it is likely to go in one direction. Whether there will again be a movement the other way is difficult of foresee. Past experience suggests that it may be so, but there are no straws aloft to permit us to gauge the wind direction and force at the present time.

Crops

For farmers occupying ordinary tillage farms the chief crop is still corn. The choice has narrowed to wheat or barley since the 1950's. Traditionally oats were a major crop, especially in the north and western regions. Indeed, the culture of oats had been sustained quite successfully throughout Britain during the depression. As late as the 1940's there were still about 3 million acres under oats. By the 1970's the area had contracted to about 600,000 acres, much of it in Scotland. The reasons for this decline are clear to see. Oats were a principal ingredient in the diet of horses, so that with the decline in their numbers throughout Britain the demand for oats fell away. Moreover, there were cultural problems with oats in the age of heavy machinery, and the old advantage of high bulk yields per acre, to compensate for the lower nutritional value, was lost as improved productivity was obtained from both wheat and barley. Oats are now grown by farmers in the lowlands, either as a catch crop from time to time or to supply specific contracts from millers particularly interested in processing oatmeal for human consumption. In the highlands the old dependence upon oats has been broken, but the crop is still in quite common cultivation to provide meal for both human and animal consumption. Other grain crops are insignificant. Rye has been a vestigial grain in British conditions for several generations and maize, which in south-eastern England enjoyed a few years of popularity during the 1970's, has not really established itself. This comparative failure is not entirely cultural; the market for English-grown maize did not develop as had been hoped. As a crop, even with improved, hardy varieties, maize must remain marginal on the northern fringes of western Europe. The other stand-by crops of the corn farmer — peas, tares, field beans — have gone the way of rye and oats into near oblivion. Their markets have disappeared and their alleged utility as cleansing crops no longer applies when agricultural science can do so much to prepare land for tillage without excessive labour. Indeed, for much of the post-war era the theoretical and practical justification of traditional rotations has been debatable, and many large-scale corn producers have contrived to manage their land with minimum interruption to the sequence of grain followed by grain.

Not all arable farming is concentrated on the production of wheat or barley. There are other crops locally of equal importance which need separate treatment. But for much of lowland Britain — indeed, from the Black Isle and Moray to the Honiton district of Devon — tillage has chiefly meant either wheat or barley so far as major cash crops are concerned. The cultivation of wheat, which shrank decisively between the 1870's and the first world war, and again in the 1920's and early 1930's , was encouraged by the government during the war and afterwards, in spite of cheap foreign supplies, partly to save on the cost of imports, partly as a strategic consideration to ensure that output should never again fall so low as it did in the early 1930's before the establishment of the Wheat Commission in 1932.

The constraints upon the growth of wheat in Britain have been considerable. The territory available for its cultivation could be increased substantially in the early 1940's, for much second-grade wheat land was still uncropped in the early years

47

of the war, but, beyond the partial re-colonisation of the ground which the Victorians had sown to wheat, the prospects were less promising. In any event, from the standpoint of 1942 or even 1950 the probable contribution of British farming to national consumption of wheat could not be expected to approach self-sufficiency. The milling industry was not especially enthusiastic about any significant increase of British wheat in the composition of bread flour, which for eighty years or more had acquired its special character from the large element of imported hard wheat in the mixture. An opportunity existed in the buoyant state of the early post-war market for cake or biscuit flour, but at that stage wheat was not regarded as an appropriate ingredient in most animal feedstuffs on account of its cost. Hard wheats had not been very successful when introduced into Britain in the past, so there seemed to be an optimum limit to the production of the crop which would not require any immense conversion of less fertile land to its cultivation. On the other hand there were factors which encouraged its greater popularity. First, new varieties not only enlarged yields to an unprecedented extent but were often suitable for less perfect growing conditions than the best pre-war varieties had required. Secondly, underdrainage of the strong clay lands preferred by wheat reduced wintertime waterlogging and carried away summer rainfall more quickly than in the past, so that the crop suffered less in the frequent wet seasons than had been the case even on fields improved by Victorian hollow-draining. Leaving aside the rather controversial issue of soil impaction caused by heavy machinery, the general trend of technical improvements in cultivation, fertilisation and harvesting was to improve yields and, less certainly, to allow the crop to be grown in more northerly districts, because its management was so much more expeditious in both soil preparation and harvesting.

The area sown to wheat probably reached a peak at some time in the early nineteenth century, before there were national statistics to record the fact, but even in 1870 there were 3·5 million acres under the crop. By 1931 the area had fallen to 1·3 million acres. Between 1943 and 1952 the acreage fluctuated around 2·1 million and then began to decline again until the mid-1960's. A steady expansion thereafter accelerated when the United Kingdom joined the EEC and resulted in as large an area under wheat (over 3·6 million acres) in 1980–81 as in 1870. But, with yields so much greater, as much wheat was produced in the post-war trough of its popularity around 1960 as in the 1860's. The decline in the area under wheat after the Korean War was the consequence of a developing world glut. Fears of long-term shortages in the post-war world had proved groundless. In Britain the spectre of the 'dollar gap' had also been laid, and this, together with a growing reluctance on the part of government to subsidise crops with substantial trading surpluses around the world, reduced demand for domestically produced wheat.

The pre-eminence of barley in the 1950's and 1960's is especially interesting. The traditional use of barley in malting was supplemented by an increased consumption in animal foodstuffs. The demand for malt grew steadily in the 1950's and 1960's, chiefly because the consumption of products made of malt was very buoyant, but partly also because imports of malt or malting barley declined in the post-war period. Better techniques of malting, improved varieties of grain suitable for cultivation in cool, temperate latitudes and some decline in the quantity of good Californian or River Plate barley on offer contributed to this domestic expansion. By the 1960's Britain had become one of the world's chief centres of barley production and a modest export trade in grain or malt had begun to develop as maltings were extended and modernised to take account of the new technology. On the other hand, these im-

Corn production in Great Britain, 1945–47 to 1980–81 (million)

	Wheat			Barley	
Average	*Acreage*	*Output (tons)*		*Acreage*	*Output (tons)*
1945–47	2·2	1·9		2·1	1·9
1950–52	2·3	2·4		2·0	2·0
1955–57	2·1	2·7		2·4	2·9
1960–62	2·0	3·2		3·6	4·9
1965–67	2·4	3·8		5·6	8·4
1970–72	2·6	4·4		5·4	8·6
1975–77	2·7	5·0		5·4	8·7
1980–81	3·6	8·5		5·6	10·3

provements made economies in the use of barley for brewing. Altogether the quantity of domestically produced barley consumed in malting averaged 0·88 million, tons (22 per cent) in 1958-59 and 1·88 million tons (21 per cent) in 1980-81. Britain had always produced a large proportion of barley barely fit for malting, which had been absorbed increasingly from the mid-nineteenth century in the production of animal feed. Concentration upon barley as the principal domestiç ingredient in meal milling was for the most part a development of the 1930's, when it was still common practice to compound feeds from mostly imported grainstuffs, above all from River Plate maize, with foreign supplies of wheatgerm, barley, pulses and even oats making up a good proportion of the remaining cereal ingredients. The war and post-war austerity brought about a change of practice, which the renewed international trade in grain of the 1950's did not undermine.

Livestock enterprises were modified to make the best use of feeds based on barley and oilseed expeller cake but balanced with many other nutriments to satisfy stock by type or age. Intensive poultry, pig and beef production in particular owed much to the availability of cheap barley, to such an extent indeed that 'barley beef' almost became an expletive in the mouths of conservationists during the 1960's. Feed barley then became a major agricultural product in itself. Many of the better new varieties brought into commercial use during the 1950's and 1960's had little appeal for the maltsters, and most of the spectacular increase in yields was achieved with feeding barleys. At the same time the price difference between wheat and the two sorts of barley narrowed until the gap between food and 'coarse' grain was often insignificant. The growers of malting grain were still to be found in the 1960's and 1970's in approximately the same locations as their forerunners a century before — Kent, East Anglia, the south and east Midlands, Yorkshire and parts of eastern Scotland. Outside the great cities, malting was especially important in places such as Ipswich, Newark, Grantham, Gainsborough and Tadcaster, near the farms from which most of the better malting grain was drawn. But barley was near enough a universal crop. Indeed, after the war its area was becoming more extensive even in the period when wheat cultivation was stable or in modest decline.

The acreage in Great Britain grew steadily from about 2 million in 1945-52 to 3·6 million in 1960-62 and 5·6 million in 1965-67, after which it stabilised but suffered no appreciable contraction when the area sown to wheat began to increase rapidly in the 1970's. In the western districts of England and Wales barley was the only crop to expand in acreage in the 1950's and early 1960's. All the increase in the arable can be attributed to the growth of barley, which increased at the expense of every other crop in mixed farming enterprises. In Scotland also the quadrupling of the acreage under barley from 0·2 million to 0·9 million acres between 1955-57 and 1975-77 was largely at the expense of other crops, chiefly oats and some rotational grass. Total output rose from 2·2 million tons in 1950-52 to 10 million tons in 1980-81. At the present time the United Kingdom has a substantial surplus of barley which must either be exported or go into intervention. That is one consequence of the great progress made in its cultivation since the war. It is also true, however, that its artificially high price has deterred compounders from making more use of the great stocks of feeding barley. Cheap supplies of exotic starch material such as tapioca have been preferred whenever available to bulk otherwise expensive cereal or compound feedstuffs. Moreover the recent depressed state of many meat-producing enterprises has reduced the absolute demand for 'sack feeds' on the farm. We cannot yet place present fluctuations properly in perspective, and it is an open question whether they will develop into trends affecting the long-run profits of barley-growing.

However, one innovation that is already so well established as to initiate a trend is the preference for winter-sown barleys. This is essentially a legacy of the the 1970's. Winter barleys were available many years before, but doubts about their resilience and productive capacity in such a wet winter climate as Britain's and obstacles to cultivation of sufficient land to accommodate all seeds in the weeks between harvest and the heavy frosts restricted the appeal of winter barley. The great efficiency of mechanised cultivation by the 1970's and the progress made by seed breeders removed both difficulties. Between 1978-79 and 1981-82 the proportion of barley sown in the autumn of the year in England and Wales rose from 34 per cent to 48 per cent of the total. In southern England, where the climate is most favourable, winter barley is now planted on a majority of fields.

Grain occupied about 50 per cent of the land in tillage in 1951 and over 60 per cent in 1981. Rotational grass had once accounted for about a third of the arable acreage, but by the latter date this proportion had fallen to a fifth. Other forage crops have since the war played a small part in tillage regimes. The turnip and its congeners now form a residual catch crop on small mixed farms in England and Wales. Two root crops, however, do remain important. At the end of the war potatoes were cultivated on about 1·2 million acres, an area that was not likely to be maintained as the economy pulled out of austerity. By 1960–62 the acreage had halved to 660,000, and it continued to diminish through the next two decades, until in 1980–81 fewer acres were sown to potatoes than to sugar beet. This diminution was partly planned by the intervention of the Potato Marketing Board, which, while it remained in being, attempted to match output to projected demand, but the fluctuations of demand for the crop were no less influential in the adjustment of acreage under potatoes.

Potatoes have always been susceptible to climatic variations, but fluctuations in yield are not matched by the volatility of demand, which is normally so unresponsive to price movements that the same acreage may produce either a glut or a dearth. On the other hand, potatoes are subject to long-run changes in the pattern of demand, since, as a cheap starch product, they tend to suffer from competition with protein-rich, more expensive or more fashionable foodstuffs as incomes rise. The trend towards fewer potatoes in human diets was marked before the war. It was reversed during the emergency and in the subsequent post-war austerity, but the decline resumed in the 1950's. Potatoes are still popular in the British diet, but the fall in acreage, supplemented by an increase in yields, has roughly kept pace with the current demand. For most of the period, indeed, the task of matching production with consumption was undertaken by the Potato Marketing Board, which could make use of several controls to regulate cultivation or distribution. Partly as an act of policy, partly by natural wastage, potato growing has become more concentrated since 1950. The number of accredited growers declined by almost two-fifths between 1950 and 1970 and the average acreage per holding increased by half. The trend is somewhat obscured by the tendency for production for sale at the farm gate to rise with the relaxation of controls, since many small farmers well placed to satisfy urban customers still grow potatoes in small lots. Throughout the period a substantial proportion of all potatoes brought to market were cultivated on holdings near the larger towns.

The largest part of the potato crop is planned to be harvested in the autumn for winter keeping. In these main-crop potatoes the United Kingdom is customarily self-sufficient. The crop is grown everywhere where climate and altitude permit. Main-crop potatoes are especially important in east central Scotland, where they form the chief cash product of arable farmers. In terms of quantity, however, about 30 per cent of the crop is produced in the eastern region of England, especially in Lincolnshire and the Fenlands. No clear geographical trend is observable in potato cultivation since the war, except perhaps the relative decline of the peat fenlands, where eelworm infestation has become very trouble-some, and a corresponding expansion in light soil areas, for example on the lower levels of the Lincolnshire wolds. The cultivation of early potatoes — that is, those varieties available for distribution in the summer months — is obviously more restricted. Earlies grown is the eastern region are ready later than those from the west, and this fact in normal years enables the market for early potatoes to be divided. The first crops are supplied from Cornwall, Pembrokeshire and Ayrshire, followed by supplies from the south coast and eventually by supplies from East Anglia, Lincolnshire and Yorkshire. Between two-thirds and three-quarters of the early potatoes consumed in Britain are home-grown. Imports, however, generally come in early in the season before Cornish or Welsh stocks are ready, although there is always some competition for the early-season markets. With integration into the EEC the risk of competition from nearby Continental sources is greater, but the pattern of supply in the past decade indicates that domestic growers have generally maintained their share of British markets.

Finally we must mention seed potatoes, which account for

about 10 per cent of the annual crop. Many farmers keep their own seed for a year or two by selecting from among their ware stocks, but there are also specialist seed producers. Seed specialists prefer districts in which the aphid population is small and less active. 'Scotch' and Ulster seed therefore has always been highly regarded, but with modern insecticides the location of seed potato production has become less restricted to the cooler, windier areas of the country. In recent years, also, imported varieties of potato seed, particularly Dutch sorts, have increased in popularity.

Part of the effort devoted to developing new varieties is directed to satisfying the demand for tubers suitable for specific purposes. Canning and freezing, especially of chipped potatoes, require certain types and quality of potatoes: crisp-making, which accounts for a substantial, and for most of the period since the mid-1950's, an increasing proportion of main-crop production, is less demanding but still affects the farmers' selection of seed and the sorting before sale of the harvested crop. Indeed, the alleged deficiencies of British potato growers have been blamed for a significant increase in imports of frozen potato products from across the Channel since the late 1970's.

The area sown to sugar beet has been tightly controlled since the war, first, by the need to supply the existing factories with an adequate but not excessive stock of raw material and, secondly, by reference to our obligations to tropical producers of cane sugar and, since 1978, EEC policy. There has been a tendency for the acreage to creep up, from 415,000 in 1945-47 to 430,000 in 1960-62, 460,000 on the eve of joining the Common Market and 560,000 in 1980-81, at the same time as average yields have increased by 30 per cent. Sugar beet remains essentially a crop of the eastern counties. In some parts of East Anglia it is still the principal arable cash crop of farmers, but at its greatest extent it is a rotational crop sown in some appropriate sequence with cereals. Its distribution has been determined partly by soil and climate, especially since it is difficult to manage in areas of high spring and autumnal rainfall, but the location of beet-processing factories, established in the 1920's and 1930's, has also had a potent influence on its cultivation because transport after harvest is relatively expensive. Since no new factories have been permitted since the 1940's the potential for cultivating the crop has been very restricted. When the Cupar factory in Scotland was closed in 1971 production virtually ceased north of the border. On the other hand the gradual extension of the area under beet has probably absorbed most of the land suitable for it in districts well placed to supply the factories still in operation. In the 1960's the British Sugar Corporation, the monopsonist processor of British sugar beet, practised a scheme of differential transport charges as a subsidy to farmers not conveniently located near one of its factories. This assistance was most effective in southern England, where farmers near the south coast found beet-growing profitable. Altogether, however, sugar beet has been grown on only about 10 per cent of holdings in England and is characteristically a product of large farms. In the 1960's more than half the crop was grown on holdings in excess of 300 acres. The tendency since the '40's has been for more concentration of production; average acreage per farm approximately doubled from under ten to over twenty between 1950 and 1970, and the number of farmers who cultivated sugar beet dropped by about two-fifths.

One constraint upon sugar beet cultivation has been its relatively high labour requirement. Around 1960, after a period of cost-saving innovation, labour still represented about one-third of total costs (almost 40 per cent of variable costs) and much was still expended on hoeing and singling in the spring and upon harvesting in the autumn. But since much of the labour input into sugar beet growing was casual and seasonal, mechanisation could reduce the wages bill considerably, and the introduction of the monogerm, pelleted seed in the 1960's virtually eliminated springtime hoeing. By the end of the decade almost all beet was planted and harvested mechanically, whereas in the mid-1950's barely half had been harvested by machine. Standard man-days per acre of sugar beet fell from seventeen in 1958 to ten in 1968 and has since fallen further to barely six in 1980–81.

Sugar beet in the late 1970's was essentially a crop of specialist arable farmers who grew it in considerable acreages and had access to large machines and substantial stocks of weedkiller and fertiliser. But one of its original advantages was in the by-products, the tops and dried pulp, which made good fodder. Thus sugar beet was popular as a crop with many eastern dairy farmers not least because its culture guaranteed cheap food for the farmers' cows. At one period pulp was offered first to the growers, and it was not always possible to buy it on the open market. The decline in small-scale beet production has not significantly deprived those livestock keepers who want it from obtaining best pulp, since many growers these days have no use for the by-product on their own farms.

Since the war there has been a considerable extension of the arable sown to vegetables, flowers and oil plants. Horticulture proper has experienced some hard knocks, particularly since the UK joined the Common Market,but it survives as an important element in land use in the Fenlands, south Lancashire and around the larger towns. The geography of market gardening has changed little since the later nineteenth century, and the essential features of its organisation similarly are the same as in the Victorian period. Smallholdings, intensively cultivated with a high degree of crop specialisation, more than half of which contain some glasshouses, prevail everywhere in the horticultural districts. Nevertheless even in these districts horticulture is commingled with orthodox tillage farming, and some crops are adaptable to field culture. So far as agriculture is concerned the boundary between field and garden production is seldom clear, but there has been a discernible trend towards large-scale cultivation of brassicas, onions, celery, carrots, peas, beans, flower bulbs in the past forty years. There are some highly specialised forms of agricultural vegetable growing. Celery, which is widespread outdoor crop on market gardens, is largely confined to the peat fens as a field crop; asparagus on a large scale is grown only on some light soil farms of the Norfolk Breckland, and flower bulbs are still a speciality of the silt fens of south Lincolnshire. Some farmers are versatile in their approach to vegetable culture. Courgettes, for example, enjoyed a brief localised vogue in eastern England as a field catch crop in the late 1970's. The mass cultivation of outdoor vegetables, however, is concentrated upon onions, carrots and the cabbage family. Although many farmers have grown one or other crop at different times, these vegetables are characteristic of the mild south-western regions, of Kent and Essex and of Lincolnshire and the Fens. In the case of carrots light soils are preferred to heavy loams or clays, and they often grow well where most other arable crops are low yielders. Most of these crops are intended for direct consumption, but there is still a demand for produce to be used in canning. Moreover a fluctuating but always substantial portion of the total output is absorbed in deep-freezing. The development of freezing has most fundamentally affected the cultivation of peas and French beans. The introduction of field contracts, arranged between food processing companies and the farmers, has resulted in a great increase in the total acreage sown to peas and beans, which are cultivated under the direct supervision of the processors.

Livestock

Livestock farming is so various that it is best described not in general terms but by reference to the principal types of animals kept on British farms. Each species of livestock requires different treatment and a different relationship with arable practices, but each also offers so many opportunities for agricultural flexibility that combinations of husbandry have in the past been very numerous. The tendency since the war for a more standardised system of animal husbandry has not resulted in a complete displacement of the older diversity.

Sheep

Sheep remain the most numerous livestock on British farms. They are the most important variety of stock kept in the highland zone, and the only farm animals -- discounting the deer kept for the small but growing trade in venison — to be found in the rough grazings. But they are a common sight both in the moorlands and high fells and in certain marshland areas of the south, where breeds such as the Romney originated. Traditionally sheep were the principal interest of agriculturists on all kinds of hill farms, where no other variety of stock-keeping was profitable, and equally they were the mainstay of many lowland regimes, especially on scarpland farms, where sheep-keeping was an integral part of corn/grass enterprises. The sheep depastured the 'seeds' which followed barley or were run, free or folded, in the roots course in order to dress the land. But with the decline of conventional rotations in the arable east the sheep lost much of its usefulness. Numbers declined in the lowlands *pari passu* with the abandonment of sub-marginal arable lands between the 1880's and the 1930's. Since the war there has been no revival in the sheep/corn husbandry in the east, because the methods and the order of tillage have changed. Sheep are still kept in the region in substantial numbers, as they can be adapted to suit different regimes in good soil districts, but the immense flocks which once characterised the Lincolnshire or Yorkshire wolds or the west Norfolk 'good sands' are now seldom seen. Even so, the counties around the Humber, together with Kent and Sussex, are the only districts in the southern lowlands in which there are forty or more sheep for each hundred acres of agricultural land. In the northern lowlands, from the vale of Tees to Aberdeenshire, the rate of stocking is somewhat greater, but it must be remembered that in these northern counties there is much hill land adjacent to the low-lying farms upon which sheep provide the only effective line of business. Apart from the moorland and mountains proper, sheep are typical of fringe areas between highland and lowland, especially in the West Midlands, the West Country and the Borders. In the southern downlands their importance has greatly declined since the war, chiefly because the old sheep walks above the traditional arable land have been ploughed and sown to crops.

Sheep farming may appear to have been an enterprise *faute de mieux* in the twentieth century. It has retreated into those parts of the country where nothing better is on offer to farmers. In the period when arable was first converted into permanent pasture sheep often increased, only to decline again in competition with cattle, particularly dairy cattle. The essential difficulty for sheep farmers is that their products have been subject to intense competition for a long period. The wool trade has fluctuated considerably in this century but the profits from wool have never been significant enough to persuade farmers to take up sheep. Nevertheless only about 12 per cent of the wool manufactured in Britain was from the domestic flock even in the comparatively buoyant period before the recession of 1973, much of it being of comparatively inferior quality suitable only for carpet weaving. Thus British wool producers have gained little benefit from the proximity of a large woollen manufacturing industry, since they have been unable to determine price levels in competition with New World suppliers. The best grade of wool cannot now be produced in Britain, where climate and vegetation are against it. In meat production the subsidiary character of British sheep farming is less evident. About half the British consumption of lamb has been provided from domestic sources since the war, and in very recent times an export trade to Europe has developed. Moreover, although a large part of the lamb eaten at British tables consists of chilled or frozen meat from the southern hemisphere, the domestic product has always commanded a premium. This, added to the different seasonal rhythm of supplies, has given British farmers a degree of protection which has not been, and is unlikely yet to be, eroded by any substantial volume of supply from nearer home, since Continental agriculture cannot provide lamb in sufficient quantity to satisfy demand elsewhere in the EEC. Sheep keeping in the lowlands has, in the past few years, been extended, so much so that the price of store lambs has risen to unprecedented levels as demand has outstripped the supply of feeding stock. But for reasons that are not entirely rational fat lamb prices have also been running at a high level.

The size of the national sheep flock has risen from 18.5 million in 1945-47 to 22.9 million in 1955-57; as high as 28.5 million in 1965-67. Thereafter there was a decline for a few years. The average in 1970-72, for example, was only 25.4 million, but this trend was reversed after Britain entered the Common Market: 27.3 million in 1975-77 and 30.7 million in 1980-81. Even in periods of a rising trend there have been years of reversal. Nineteen-forty-seven, for instance, saw a decline in the national flock of more than 3.5 million owing to the adverse season. The great majority of the sheep are kept extensively, that is, in free-running flocks usually on permanent pasture. Close folding, the preferred method of depasturing fallow-break crops, had largely disappeared by the 1950's because it is so expensive of labour, and in lowland enterprises sheep are nowadays usually allowed to range freely over grassland or leys. Until recent years the indoor management of sheep, even in winter lambing, was regarded either as eccentric or as too expensive to be practicable, but the advantages of providing some shelter have been proved and sheep housing is becoming quite common on the larger farms, especially in the lowlands. One problem is that the average size of British flocks is too small to make full use of the new techniques of management. Few experts would recommend a flock of less than 500 head, but fewer than 10 per cent of all flocks in Britain exceed that figure and in many extensive upland pastures the rate of stocking is very low, since in an unimproved state such grassland can support few animals upon the thin vegetation growing naturally. In such widespread, often intermixed, enterprises sheep housing is almost unthinkable and lambing has to be delayed until the weather will allow the young stock to survive in tolerable numbers. Even in prosperous times sheep farming in the highland zone is precarious and losses are substantial. As a rule, hill sheep farmers have survived only because of the special subsidy payable on breeding ewes in areas where fattening is difficult or impossible. In north-western Scotland, for example, nearly all the graziers' money income in the 1950's and 1960's apparently came from the hill-farm subsidies.

Pigs

Pig-keeping has tended to be the most volatile type of animal husbandry. It has even fluctuated more widely than the poultry trade since the war. Because the pig is very fecund and the average sow will produce two litters a year, animal numbers will inevitably vary a great deal, since any substantial slaughter of sows and gilts must reduce the offspring available for fattening, but, by the same token, numbers can be replaced quickly when prospects seem more appealing. Pig-keeping is conventionally divided into two branches, according to the product. The bacon trade has always been partly satisfied by imports. The art of producing good bacon at a price to compete with Danish or Irish imports is more difficult than the art of feeding pigs for the pork trade. The bulk of the pork and processed pork poducts consumed in Britain is obtained from domestic sources, but demand has not always been constant enough to assure farmers of good profits, despite the degree of protection they enjoy. The bacon producers, however, have enjoyed rather worse fortunes since the 1930's. Home production increased by only about a-quarter between 1938 and 1967, although demand *per capita* grew not at all. There has therefore been a modest saving on imports, but, in terms of both output and stock numbers the management of pigs for bacon has slipped well behind the other branch of the trade.

Pig-keeping has always been ancillary to other species of husbandry. The usefulness of the pig as a scavenger or in consuming the surplus produce of dairying and even of arable farming has given it a universal status in the farmyard. In the past also, at least as late as the 1950's, cottage pig-keeping was widespread. Since much of the produce from these domestic pigsties was consumed directly in the home, a proportion of the output of pig-keepers escaped notice in official statistics. Nevertheless, for upwards of a century there has been a relatively small number of large-scale pork or bacon producers whose herds numbered dozens, perhaps hundreds, of animals. The long-standing connection of pig-keeping with dairying has not been completely broken, but the traditional dependence of swine upon buttermilk or whey has declined with the decay of farm-based butter and cheese-making. The county statistics, however, have for twenty years suggested that pig-keeping on a commercial scale is more usually located in arable districts, especially in Yorkshire and East Anglia, rather than in the western pastoral region, although there are districts of concentration in Lancashire, north Shropshire and west Cornwall comparable to Norfolk and Essex. Since pigs are not often kept outdoors on grass, the correlation of stock numbers with pasture is low. As livestock they fit in well with tillage regimes, and the trend towards bulk housing of pigs has rather reinforced the place of the arable farmer in the affluent lowlands.

The number of pigs recorded in the agricultural statistics has risen very much since the war, from 1·6 million in 1945-47 to 5·2 million in 1960-62 and 7·4 million in 1970-72. Since 1973 growth has been erratic, with the result that by 1980-81 there were fewer pigs, 7·2 million, in Great Britain than there had been a decade earlier. Numbers tend to fluctuate from year to year, but, in the absence of a large demand for British pork on the Continent, and with high input costs, the expansion of the 1950's and 1960's is not likely to be repeated. Domestic demand for pork doubled between the 1930's and 1960's, but further increases upon the 26 lb per head achieved by 1965 have been difficult to consolidate. On the other hand, the efficiency of pig-keeping has been greatly improved since the war. The number of holdings with pigs halved in the fifteen years before 1970, and by that date fewer than 30 per cent of all holdings in Britain reported any pigs in the annual statistics. Expressed more graphically, the four-to-fivefold increase in pig numbers between 1945 and 1970 was accommodated on less than a third of the holdings keeping pigs at the former date. In other words, pig-keeping changed from a sideline on the majority of general mixed farms to an enterprise as nearly industrialised as is possible in agriculture. About half of all the pigs recorded by 1970 were managed in herds of 200 or more, especially in the eastern lowlands, where herds of more than 1,000 are not uncommon. Nevertheless, even then, most holdings kept herds of fewer than fifty pigs, ranging from 40-45 per cent in the south and east of England to three-quarters or more in the north and west, in Wales and much of Scotland. Even in the south-east less than a-quarter of enterprises possessed herds of over 200 head, but this illustrates the capital-intensive nature of much commercial pig production. In the east substantial herds have been accumulated by arable farmers who have been able, for much of the period, to make savings on the cost of feed by supplying barley meal direct to the pig sheds. On many of the tillage farms in which stock-keeping has been retained the pig rather than the bullock or the sheep has become the chief concern. Its fecundity and rapid fattening offer advantages, particularly in an inflationary and changeable period, but the larger the enterprise the less versatile the structure of pig-keeping becomes, since expensive housing, farrowing and feed installations have to be maintained in use in all but the most adverse circumstances. Many of the more commercially-minded arable farmers have concentrated upon fattening for pork or manufactured pig meat, but this has meant that breeding has become a specialist branch equally susceptible to the vagaries of the market.

Beef Cattle

After dairying the most important segment of British agriculture for most of the period since the war has been beef production, which in the 1960's accounted for over 15 per cent of all farm sales. In the twenty years after 1950 production rose by more than 50 per cent. Although the underlying trend of growth has been much less marked since entry into the Common Market, bullock-fattening remains a principal interest of farmers in many arable regimes. The production of beef is not, of course, confined to the feeding of bullocks as a specialist enterprise. Much beef, often of inferior quality, has always come from animals not bred directly for meat, above all from breeding and dairy stock. Equally, beef husbandry is still often relatively less specialised by enterprise than other types of pastoral activity. To some extent the long-standing division between west and east in rearing and fattening persists, but changes in tillage have modified the pattern, because arable farmers in the east have fewer supplies of forage material than in the nineteenth alnd early twentieth centuries. Moreover, although government subsidies encouraged production, the disaggregated system of distribution, at least until the Meat and Livestock Commission attempted to regulate the trade, worked against the convergence of practical management and coherent economics. Until the 1970's even the statistical information about beef-cattle enterprises was inconsistent, since breeding stocks were not distinguished by type and the difference between store and fat cattle was seldom clarified.

From the later 1960's, however, the general situation is quite clear. Thus about three-quarters of home-bred cattle for beef were supplied by dairy enterprises from culled cows or bulls and surplus calves, many of which were sold to be run on by other farmers or graziers. Many dairy farmers cater to the beef market by cross-breeding with beef cattle a selection of their cows, with the result that much of the meat produced as a subsidiary enterprise to dairying is of quality equal to that supplied by the specialists with Aberdeen Angus, Hereford, Charolais or beef-cross breeds. Many of these specialists in beef production command great prestige, but the output of such enterprises, large and small, probably accounted for less than a fifth of the total in 1970. The dual-purpose breeds, especially the Shorthorns, so popular in the nineteenth century had largely disappeared by the 1960's.

Beef production is difficult to define clearly because it is widely practised as a by-product of other agricultural enterprises. On the stores side of the business there are rather more graziers whose principal interest is in cattle breeding, but in the fattening trade most of the singular concerns appear to be in the hands of elderly, sometimes retired, farmers who are prepared to forgo maximum profits for ease of management. So far as one can judge, the fattening trade at least is extensively divided. The herds are quite small and inconstant, since bullock feeding depends so much upon the buying in of stores, and the decision whether to increase or reduce such purchases is taken in the light of prevailing conditions, partly in ruling prices but chiefly in fodder supplies. The best land suitable for keeping cattle has in the twentieth century been selected for dairying. In the lowlands beef cattle have seldom been profitable enough on their own to set the pattern of agriculture, but, since they can be employed very flexibly to supplement most other species of farming, purchased stores (more extensively than home-breds) were at least until the later 1960's almost universal in arable, dairying and many mixed systems of husbandry outside the highland zone. Everything conspired to promote versatility: subsidisation was not founded upon any system of licences or quotas; markets were ubiquitous, were well supplied with calves or stores and could also handle the fatstock produced locally for diffusion into the national system of consumption. In addition, although elaborate purpose-built fixed equipment was employed in cattle-keeping it was not necessary when the majority of farmsteads possessed sufficient buildings and fold-yards to provide adequate shelter.

The situation about 1950 cannot be reconstructed with accuracy. Two features need to be emphasised, however. First, beef production was apparently less intimately bound up with dairying. Dairy farmers contributed much by way of calf sales and culled cows, but the system of intensive mixed husbandry in the eastern and north-eastern counties had not been modified almost out of existence by new rotations. Fallow-break forage crops were still commonly cultivated, and a substantial quantity of cereal, potato and sugar beet by-products was garnered even in conditions of wartime emergency. Thus bullock fattening was still a cornerstone of much corn and root arable husbandry. It had survived better through the inter-war years in depressed districts of East Anglia and Lincolnshire, thanks in part to a plentiful supply of Irish stores. The second point to be stressed, however, is that wartime planning attempted to promote arable production at the expense of pastoral in the regions apt for tillage. Livestock, which competed with humans for scarce food supplies, required the occupation of precious shipping space and was expensive to produce in terms of comparative food values, was given a low priority. Thus after the war it was necessary to subsidise the restoration and expansion of the beef trade in agriculture, although the objectives of policy were not entirely clear, given the commitment to the Commonwealth.

The number of cattle kept in Great Britain, including the dairy herd, stood at 8·1 million in 1939. From 1945 to 1950 the national herd increased from 8·7 million to 9·4 million. Thereafter there was a rapid expansion — 1960, 10·8 million; 1970, 11·3 million; 1975, 13·1 million — but it had fallen back by 1980 to about 11·9 million. The national beef herd numbered perhaps 3 million at the latter date, including cows and heifers used in suckling calves, intended for slaughter. It has usually been assumed that about 40 per cent of the aggregate number of cattle is slaughtered every year. The proportion oscillates from season to season, but the trend seems to have been reasonably consistent through several decades. A better guide is the data of beef and veal prepared for consumption from home stocks, since there was always some variation in the size or type of cattle brought to the abbatoir. Before the war the average production of beef in the United Kingdom was 580,000 tons. After a fall in the earlier 1940's, the output achieved in the late 1930's was matched by 1945-51. In 1959-61 production had risen to 780,000 tons, in

1969-71 to 980,000 tons, and reached a peak of 1,215,000 tons in 1975. But despite rising real incomes *per capita*, consumption of beef had not increased: in 1936-38 it was about 55 lb, in 1964-66 48 lb and in 1978-79 under 45 lb. By comparison with the 1920's and 1930's there was a long-term decline in the quantity of imported beef placed on the British market, however, from about 55 per cent to about 25 per cent of total consumption. Imports have therefore borne the brunt of the long-run contraction of demand, although farmers at home have at times felt the effects of glut in their profit margins.

The fattening of beef has undergone several important changes since the war. The traditional method was to prepare the beasts for market at about three years old. But feeding up to prime fatness was usually confined to the last few months of the life cycle, when the animals were put out to the best grass in summer, or fed on hay, cereals or concentrates in winter. The system was fully adapted to orthodox regimes of tillage and mixed husbandry but could be made to work in other surroundings provided that sufficient pasturage was available for 'keeping'. It was hallowed by tradition, but could be justified on the grounds that consumers in general preferred mature beef. It remained the dominant practice of feeding beef cattle into the 1950's. But with the decline of traditional rotations and a growing cost-consciousness among farmers, the disadvantages of the method became apparent. Subsidies were granted for beasts ready for the market, and farmers could obtain them quicker if they adopted different practices. Various methods, tried experimentally in the 1920's and 1930's, were severally adopted in the 1950's and 1960's. All enabled farmers to sell fatstock at two years of age or less, and most did not put them to much inconvenience in finding new capital equipment. One system which became notorious in the mid-1960's was the production of beef by intensive feeding of barley to Friesian calves to fatten them within the year. It was widely adopted only by the great arable farmers of the east and south, who produced a large surplus of barley and who had the resources to build the intensive fattening sheds needed for enclosed management. It depended upon the comparative cheapness of barley and upon the advantageousness of beef production by comparison with other forms of husbandry. It had passed its meridian by 1965 and was seldom employed as a method in its own right after the great dearth of cereals in 1972. More conventional is the semi-intensive, eighteen-month system, which evolved out of the older practice of finishing from half-fat within a season. Calves born in summer or autumn are grazed on good pasture the following summer and fed intensively in the winter. They come up for slaughter variously between December and April, when the demand for beef is at its highest point in the year. This method has been very successful, but because it is comparatively demanding of concentrates it has tended to be modified so as to reduce the period of intensive feeding since the mid-1970's, when the price of concentrates increased so much.

Poultry

Poultry-keeping on farms has undergone a profound change since the 1950's. In essence it is now the best example of factory farming in Britain. As a result there has been a long-run decline in the real price of both eggs and poultry meat. Poultry includes fowls, turkeys, geese and ducks, but 95 per cent of the national flock in the 1960's and 1970's consisted of fowls and under 4 per cent of turkeys. In fowl-keeping there have developed three distinct branches of activity, breeding, egg-laying and meat production. When most birds were kept in small 'barn door' flocks there was little or no specialisation. The first stage in the evolution of a poultry industry, therefore, was the separation of function among poultry-keepers. In the inter war years large enterprises were formed, and in Sussex and Lancashire especially they became highly specialised, with few interests outside the poultry trade. Even so, most poultry keepers still produced both eggs and meat, setting aside part of their capacity to fatten capons or hens to eke out the income received for eggs. Even breeding was not yet wholly separated from commercial activities. The bulk of the output in the 1930's came from small, subsidiary flocks, so that poultry-keeping was not only a consuming interest of many cottage smallholders but was also virtually universal on mixed farms. Since the mid-1950's specialisation has proceeded far. Breeding has become concentrated in few hands; in the mid-

1960's, for example, fewer than 200 holdings held half the breeding stock, and about a dozen companies controlled most of the output. Moreover, egg-laying birds and broiler stock have normally been kept separate on different holdings. At the same time interest in the various species of poultry also became concentrated on specialist holdings, although distribution of fatstock has tended to be controlled by a small number of substantial companies.

Egg production was the main line of business for commercial keepers from the 1920's to the late 1950's, but near saturation of demand for eggs then caused a change of direction. Egg production was revolutionised by the adoption of the battery system of management in place of 'deep litter' or 'folding' systems. The latter were rather less productive in terms of output even in favourable conditions than batteries, and they were distinctly less attractive to farmers when labour costs were compared. Battery housing, however, is even more capital-intensive than deep-litter housing, and successful poultry enterprises have tended to become ever larger as costs have risen. The result has been polarisation of egg production. In the 1950's and early 1960's two-thirds of producers supplied less than thirty dozen eggs per week and under 2 per cent more than ten boxes (300 dozen). By the late 1970's 15 per cent of enterprises were in the category of large-scale producers and under 60 per cent among the smallest. The chief casualty has been the medium-sized enterprise with between 100 and 2,000 birds. In 1968, for instance, 70 per cent of birds were kept in holdings with fewer than 100 head, and half in units of over 5,000 head. The trend observed in the 1960's has continued, not least because small-scale producers have been able to dispose of their production quickly and cheaply at the farm gate. The bigger commercial outlets have been served by the large-scale producers, even though some, like the Eastwood concern, failed amid accelerating inflation in the 1970's. The concentration of the industry since the mid-1960's has not meant that these large companies have become more numerous, merely that they have held their position in a period of declining participation in the egg trade among landholders at large.

Meat production has seen a very similar rate of technical

development since the 1950's, when poultry feeding was first encouraged as a source of cheap protein at the end of rationing. The trade became highly specialised as rapid fattening of broilers was accepted by producers as the most cost-effective means of producing cheap poultry meat. New hybrid strains fed on complex compound feed will fatten out at 3½–4 lb in six weeks. By comparison with the 6 lb capon preferred in the early 1950's, costs were reduced by half to two-thirds per bird by the 1960's. Marketing of the new broiler was successful, and in order to supply the seemingly insatiable demand for roasting fowls in the 1960's the industry expanded quickly into the same kind of industrialised production as in the egg trade. Capital intensity is necessary because the initial outlay on specialised buildings is high. In 1960, for example, a 10,000 bird broiler house cost £7,000 (almost twice the average price of a three-bedroom house), but four or five batches of birds could be put through in a year, and labour costs on such purpose-built sites were minimal until the time of slaughter.

By the early 1970's the United Kingdom held 50 million broilers and capons, of which at least three-quarters were birds intended to be killed at 4 lb in weight or less. This was eight times more than the average for 1955–57 and double the numbers produced in the mid-1960's. By 1980 the broiler flock stood at 60 million. Clearly the age of expansion had passed by the mid-1970's, although in the past fifteen years much effort has been spent in promoting other kinds of poultry meat, especially turkey, and consumption *per capita* remains on a high plateau. Before the watershed of 1972–73 the current price of fowls fell steadily from 24p per lb in 1955–57 to a low point of 15p in 1967–69. In real terms the price continued to fall gently throughout the 1970's.

The total number of registered poultry keepers supplying either eggs or meat fell steadily from the 1950's to the 1970's, with a specially sharp decline in the 1960's. The number of commercial flocks declined between 1960 and 1975 by more than half, to number about 130,000. The location of the two trades is still influenced by tradition. Thus the north-west, centred upon Lancashire, and the south-east, in Surrey and Sussex, are still very important, but poultry keeping is not dependent upon soil or market location and has become widely dispersed around Britain since the war, with parts of the arable eastern region showing evidence of growth in the 1950's, not least because poultry-keeping could be combined easily with full-time arable farming. These holdings have obviously diminished in number since 1960 but not in greater proportion than in the older centres of the business.

Dairying

Dairying is the most important livestock enterprise and one of the most important branches of agriculture as a whole. In 1960-61, for instance, about 23 per cent by value of all agricultural output was contributed by dairying, that is to say, £350 million. Between 1937-38 and 1960-61 gross output almost doubled in quantity, and the rise continued throughout the 1960's. Nevertheless the share of dairying declined slightly from rather above to rather below 25 per cent of the total. It reached a peak of 30 per cent of gross output at the end of the war, when milk production had been encouraged in order to increase the supply of liquid milk for reasons of public health. Even so, total production was enlarged only from 1·38 million gals. to 1·61 million between 1937-38 and 1944-47 — modest beside the 50 per cent increase in the next fifteen years. The number of cows and heifers in milk or in calf increased from about 4 million in 1946 to 4·5 million in 1960 and 4.87 million in 1970. The dairy herd, so called in the statistics, was not separately enumerated before the mid-1950's: excluding in-calf heifers, the numbers increased from 2·8 million in 1955-57 to 3·08 million in 1970-72 and then declined slightly to 2·9 million in 1980-81.

In the past century dairying has concentrated upon the production of liquid milk. In the 1960's two-thirds of milk production was sold for direct consumption and less than a quarter was destined for manufacture,a proportion that was rather less than in the 1930's. Even though there have been changes since the UK entered the EEC, it remains true that the characteristic and distinguishing feature of dairying since the network of railways was constructed has been the importance of the liquid milk trade. One consequence has been a large interest in winter-produced milk, a relatively expensive commodity that can be dispensed with in butter and cheese-making enterprises. The fixation upon liquid milk reflected both the very large urban demand for the product early in the century and the difficulty of competing with cheap imports of butter and cheese. The perishability of liquid milk not only offered great protection to British dairy farmers in the era of open markets for food but also allowed others who had not been engaged in dairying to take up the business. Districts in the east and south-east of England which in the mid-nineteenth century had had very few commercial dairy herds re-entered the business between the 1880's and the 1920's. This development, important for the management of parti-cular holdings, was of marginal significance at large, since most of the real increase in both herd numbers and output occurred in traditional dairy districts or in areas once too remote for large-scale commercial dairying — the far western district of England, for example, which benefited from more rapid transport in the twentieth century. The immense market of London assisted the development of dairying in the eastern counties where, however, climate and terrain discouraged the growth of early spring grass and often caused summer pastures to dry out, so that many farmers found it expedient to concentrate on winter milk, not least because feeding-stuffs were readily available from surplus arable products. The revival of dairying in the south-eastern quadrant of England, often under the guidance of expatriates from western Scotland or the dairy districts of England, had been most vigorous before the 1920's. In the first year in which detailed production data were collected, 1924-25, 25 per cent of total milk sales originated in the eastern, southern and south-eastern districts; by 1966-67 the percentage had fallen to 17. By the latter date output was barely sufficient to satisfy local, non-metropolitan demand in the region. The proportional decline was especially rapid in the 1960's; by the early 1970's output from the southern arable counties hardly equalled 10 per cent of the total.

The traditional dairying districts retain their leadership of the industry. Four regions are dominant at the present as they were one and two centuries ago. Cheshire and its adjacent counties, corresponding more or less exactly to the north-western region of the Milk Marketing Board, possess a fifth of all dairy cattle and supply over a fifth of milk output. Secondly, there is the south-western dairy district — Dorset, Somerset and Wiltshire — with perhaps 15 per cent of dairy cattle; thirdly, south-west Wales, around Carmarthen, and, fourthly, south-west Scotland, above all Ayrshire. In all, soil, climature and traditional skills combined to provide ideal conditions. Each region made the transfer from butter or cheese-making to liquid milk production without much difficulty once the means of distribution had been created, and each has more or less successfully withstood the temptation for farmers to plough up their first-rate permanent pasture for corn. Other regions, the far western district of England, Devon and Cornwall, north Wales and Cumbria, have considerable dairy herds and numerous cattle enterprises. Dairying is, and long has been, the chief interest of farmers in the western pastoral region below an altitude of about 500 ft, in its river valleys and broader plains on both clay and loam soils. The increasing importance of the west as a whole was marked between 1950 and 1965, when output increased by almost 30 per cent and the numbers of cows by over 13 per cent, whereas in the east output grew by about 6 per cent from fewer cows.

In England and Wales dairy cows have always been kept on a diversity of holdings; in Scotland the national herd tends to be more concentrated. Nevertheless in England and Wales 75 per cent of dairy cows were found on dairy farms in 1965 and 89 per cent in Scotland. The average size of the herd on dairy farms in Scotland in 1965 was 44, and 34 south of the Border. These herds had almost doubled in average numbers since the war and continued to increase in the 1970's. The number of dairy farms declined steadily throughout the 1950's and 1960's. Registered milk producers numbered 170,000 in 1950, 131,000 in 1960 and 86,000 in 1970. By 1980 there were only about 50,000 holdings with dairy cattle in Britain.

Before the war the development of the trade in liquid milk depended upon the extension of the rural network of railways. The great urban agglomerations had an almost insatiable appetite for milk, and wholesale merchants had increasingly to search for supplies farther afield, especially when, as between London, Bristol and Birmingham, there was competition for the produce of particular districts. When the trade was buoyant the merchants had to find supplies wherever they could, but when, as in the 1930's, the milk trade was slack it was the farmers, even in remote parts such as Galloway, who looked to London to take their surplus and at prices which even undercut wholesale milk prices current in south-eastern England. By the 1920's and 1930's, therefore, the tentacles of the metropolitan markets had reached far out into the dairy districts throughout Britain, but the pattern of marketing was erratic and disorderly. The Milk Marketing Board attempted to remedy this situation. Price control was one instrument of regulation, another was the evolution of bulk milk collection by road tanker, organised by the MMB and fully developed by the 1950's. In this system both large and small producers have been served equally through the operation of regular collection rounds. Moreover the allocation of milk between direct consumption and manufacturing could be determined on a rational anlysis of the market, impossible in the fragmented distribution of the 1920's.

Manufactured milk products — butter, cheese, condensed milk, yoghurt, dried milk powder, sterilised cream, etc. — have accounted for 20-30 per cent of gross output since the war. This is a much smaller proportion than in other European countries, but the percentage, although inclined to fluctuate, remained broadly the same for a long period, beginning to rise only after 1973 as a trend. In Britain cheese has traditionally been the most important of these manufactures, but only about a tenth of milk production has customarily been converted into cheese. All these processed products are manufactured out of substantial summer surpluses, especially in the western counties, where virtually all the creameries and milk factories are situated. From Strathclyde to Cornwall between a third and a half of all milk has consistently been sold for processing since the later 1950's. There are many advantages in using summer milk for manufacturing, not least its cheapness. The relatively expensive winter milk has to be used for direct consumption, because supplies are barely equal to demand between October and April. In the west, where processing into butter or cheese is an ancient art, a considerable if variable proportion of the surplus has, since the war at least, been converted into milk powder or condensed for canning. In the past two decades the trade in flavoured yoghurts has increased wonderfully, and several even newer products have added much-needed variety to the creamery business. Manufacturing output has more or less kept pace with the expansion of total milk production. The quantity available for processing rose from almost 300 million gallons in 1933-37 to over 500 million gallons in 1965-70, or by about 50 per cent, whereas gross output increased by almost 90 per cent. Since 1973 the proportion of milk sent for manufacturing has increased by at least 15 per cent more than total output, a fair proportion of which has been destined simply for intervention storage.

The traditional drawback of milk processing has been foreign competition. Cheap butter, cheap condensed milk and, to a less extent, cheap cheese, from the Commonwealth, from the United States and from Europe, reduced incentives to enlarge the share of the market supplied from British factories. Had there been a means of absorbing the summer surplus in the west without manufacturing it into butter, cheese, etc., the business would probably have declined further after 1860. An absolute minimum between a fifth and a quarter of output must, however, be processed or destroyed. Despite the increase of production during this century this proportion remains. Only since declining *per capita* consumption combined with stagnant population growth in the 1970's has the surplus notably increased. After 1973 oversea supplies from many Commonwealth and EFTA sources diminished, but the opportunity for greater manufacturing self-sufficiency at home was limited because the EEC countries had themselves well established and efficient milk processing industries for which the British market became a prime target. The United Kingdom imported over 90 per cent of butter and over 50 per cent of cheese consumed in 1965; the proportions by 1980 were 80 per cent and 45 per cent respectively, even though the sources of produce were very different.

5 · Marketing

A recurrent problem in agriculture has been the marketing of produce. For sixty years before 1940 it was a constant complaint among agriculturists that oversea competition had undermined the commercial foundations of British food production. This was a plea for tariff protection, which until the 1930's fell on deaf ears, and also an acknowledgement, usually oblique, that the system of distribution of commodities was deficient or unnecessarily cumbersome. The second argument became more insistent in the 1930's. The outcome was the partial reorganisation of agricultural marketing and a wider acceptance of the principle of monopsony in order to rationalise the commodity trade, even before the war imposed new discipline in agricultural distribution. In essence the argument rested on two different premises: first that market organisation was defective and secondly that, in the absence of supervision, the quality and trading standards of agricultural produce were too diverse and too variable to assure the consumers' loyalty. In the different context of the EEC free-trade area both points are still made. The disorganisation of producers and the lack of objective standards for their products have been blamed for the poor performance of British agriculture in selling bacon, cheese, tomatoes and other salad crops, hard fruit and, at times, even potatoes, by comparison with various competitors. Some complaints — about bacon, for instance — have been repeated from decade to decade with little variation of emphasis.

Traditionally farmers traded their produce piecemeal through local markets or middlemen who collected wholesale parcels from a number of suppliers. The pattern of marketing began to change in the nineteenth century with the spread of railways. The markets, however, were influenced much more strongly by buyers than by sellers, because for a whole range of agricultural commodities merchants, processors and distributors were better organised than the farmers, who were slow to take advantage of co-operative marketing. Very few farmers, at least before the 1960's, were able to turn out any product in sufficient quantity to deal on equal terms with the wholesalers. From the late nineteenth century concentration in processing and distribution proceeded fast. Flour milling, compounding, biscuit-making (and later large-scale bread-making), malting and brewing, the milk trade and to a less marked extent the mass organisation of the domestic meat trade were all controlled by large enterprises before 1914. The process has continued to the present time. To rub salt in farmers' wounds, the mass organisation of distribution was often built up to regulate supplies of oversea produce within the domestic market. Before the 1930's there was comparatively little that farmers could do to counteract this oligopsony. The railways proved to be a two-edged weapon, for, much as they enlarged domestic outlets for farmer's produce, they also brought even cheaper goods on to the market from overseas. On the other hand the rationalisation of the system of public markets and private sales had allowed economies of scale to be made in domestic distribution. Many fewer markets and fairs were active in the 1930's than in the 1830's, while selling by sample was virtually ubiquitous for suitable commodities.

For farmers the pattern of marketing in the 1930's was both discrete and diffuse. Prices were fixed almost without reference to the state of domestic supplies, and in periods of abundance farmers found that their produce was not wanted, since processors and commodity merchants were committed to foreign supplies, often because they were better adapted to the prevailing market. Domestic agriculture did not fully respond to changing schedules of demand and was thus left aground by fluctuations of taste. Here there is a danger of exaggeration; between 1880 and 1940 British agriculture displayed much versatility in adjusting to new production. Yet by the end of the long depression agriculture was out of joint with the state of the food industries. Several writers called for radical reform of marketing in the inter-war years and, although not all the proposals put forward were then adopted, the trend of the argument was consistent enough to form the basis of pre-war innovation and post-war consolidation.

The essential difficulty was to co-ordinate the allocation of agricultural produce on the market (and, where necessary, to create or refine demand for such produce) and the protection of farmers' interests, above all their income, without raising prices so much as to deter consumption. But there was another factor in the equation; it was usually necessary also to improve the quality or acceptability of most agricultural commodities. It was widely believed in the 1930's as in the 1950's that a standardised product, preferably one bearing an official seal of approval, would be easier to sell than the commodities thrown on the market straight from the farm. Organising, regulating, levelling were the watchwords of the campaign for official, and therefore benign, oligopoly. In effect, however, the marketing of livestock proved too difficult to regulate by a public agency, and the trade in corn, although subject to some government subvention, was overshadowed by dealing on the international exchanges. For several less important commodities — wool sugar, hides, butter — British output was too small and British demand too high for domestic production to determine prevailing price levels. Attempts to organise marketing were therefore either half-hearted or unsuccessful until the war. Some products were protected by their perishability, but that was perhaps small comfort for growers who could not capitalise upon local dearths although they were often stricken by local gluts. Regulating the trade in horticultural commodities and in eggs proved very difficult even in the 1940's during the years of severe rationing.

On the Continent much progress was made before the 1930's in protecting the farmer and grower through elaborate schemes of co-operation. But whereas peasants were not averse from pooling their resources in Denmark, Belgium or Germany, British farmers apparently found the idea impracticable or distasteful. Few co-operatives flourished before the 1960's, and what success can be reported was achieved in purchasing rather than selling organisations, since farmers seem to have been more prepared to ' buy their seeds or fertilisers from outside the orthodox commercial channels of supply than to sell their portion of grain, potatoes, carcase meat or eggs in such a way. One reason for this reluctance must be that, for all its defects, the system of agricultural marketing, and not least its domination by the large commercial enterprises, was better organised and less inimical to the farmer than on the Continent. Another, less directly appropriate to the present discussion, is that the landlord-tenant system was still strong enough to stunt the growth of farmers' commercial organisations.

In the 1930's the marketing problems of agriculture were eased to a limited extent by tariffs or import controls, although, in making arrangements to protect the Empire from too sharp a contraction of demand for its multifarious primary products in the mother country, the government muted the effects of protectionism upon domestic agriculture. A more characteristic solution was the establishment of Marketing Boards, representing the interests of producers but also answerable to consumers and politicians, which, it was believed, would reorganise trade, stabilise prices and enlarge consumption. The Marketing Board has been a feature of agricultural planning ever since. Agencies of similar constitution have developed in other sophisticated economies to control the distribution of primary products. They stand out as durable monuments to what the Americans call New Deal thinking in economic management. They could perform no useful function in the command economy of the 1940's, but otherwise have been adapted to serve agriculture through several vicissitudes of government intervention and remain in being within the constitution of the CAP when some at least of the principles upon which the Milk Marketing Board are managed fly in the face of Common Market notions of internal free trade.

In the 1930's four Marketing Boards were established. These schemes were voluntary, although successful Boards soon made it difficult for producers to remain outside, so comprehensive were they in bringing together supplies and fixing price levels. During the war, when the Boards were actually in suspension, the foundations laid in the few years of operation before 1939 were extended and the superstructure of controlled marketing rose to heights hardly forecast in the early days. But the two best organised Boards, for milk and hops, had already devised methods of predicting and regulating supplies, and of distributing the produce, that were of immense value to the Ministry of Food in the 1940's. In turn the Boards, when they were refounded, could build up the organisation inherited from the Ministry.

The Board for hops was the first to be established. It proved very effective chiefly because of the small number of growers involved. It controlled the market by purchasing all hops sold and restricted production by acreage quotas, which were used to exclude newcomers. Moreover the Board was supported by heavy duties on imports and by closely supervised import quotas. The Hop Marketing Board exemplified the inter-relationship of self-regulation and government intervention as the best guarantee of success. The Potato Marketing Board attempted in a more diffuse way to control production by quotas and fines for exceeding the permitted acreage. The problem was that potatoes were much more difficult to manage through a regulatory agency. Catch cropping was hard to eradicate and quality difficult to maintain. One method attempted to control quality by specifying a minimum size for potatoes to be sold through the Board. The Potato Marketing Board had few difficulties with imports in the 1930's, but its success from the growers' point of view was modest. The least satisfactory of these early Boards was that set up to regulate the trade in bacon pigs, which failed to negotiate stable prices, owing, in part, to the elastic demand for bacon and, in part, to the high level of imports. Bacon, in other words, enjoyed little natural protection, and the government was unwilling to impose deterrent tariffs on oversea supplies. The Board was not revived after wartime suspension.

But the greatest success was in the marketing of milk. Four district Boards were established, one for England and Wales and three for different parts of Scotland, although their cons-titutions were virtually the same. The Milk Marketing Boards were charged with the task of equalising the price of liquid milk across the country, since cut-throat competition had been no less disturbing than chronically low prices in the 1920's and early 1930's. A higher, more remunerative price for milk was gradually achieved as more and more substantial producers were drawn into the schemes. One reason for this success was the stabilisation of markets for milk used in manufacturing, thus removing the temptation to divert surpluses into the liquid trade. The Boards re-established a firm base for butter and cheese-making and for milk processing, although imports remained an obstacle before the war. A secondary effect of the Boards' intervention in producers' concerns was a notable improvement in milk hygiene and freedom from disease. The campaign was not solely the responsibility of the MMB's, but their refusal to deal in contaminated milk was probably more effective than scientific exhortations. The pre-war Boards, however, were not the large-scale commercial undertakings familiar in later times. Their functions were essentially regulatory and negotiating. We cannot be certain that they would have developed extensive commercial activities without the wartime experience of physical controls. They were scarcely launched before the onset of war.

The Boards, subsumed under the Ministries of Food and Agriculture throughout the 1940's, were not refounded until after 1954. Direct administration of centrally determined prices and production targets continued to be necessary in the period of acute shortages after the war. But it is also true that centralised planning was more congenial to the Labour governments of 1945 and 1950, and even to the farmers whose views were expressed through the NFU, since experience had suggested that the command economy had produced very favourable results for agriculture. The Korean War delayed the movement away from centralised planning, but with the end of rationing for all foodstuffs in 1954 some structure that would protect farmers was urgently required. Three Marketing Boards were therefore revived, and new ones were instituted for eggs, wool, tomatoes and cucumbers. The constitutions of the three Boards were virtually unaltered, and the three new ones were constructed in the same way, allowing for the difference in the commodities to be marketed.

The Milk Marketing Boards have grown enormously since their refoundation and some new functions have been added to those performed in the 1930's. The Boards were designed to take account of the prevalent economics of dairying. Most milk was, and continues to be, produced in order to satisfy the demand for liquid supplies, but there has always been a surplus available for manufacturing. The effective price structure of the two commodities differs somewhat, since there is no natural protection for butter, cheese or yoghurt, and prices for manufacturing milk generally rule lower than the price for fresh liquid milk. The Board has contrived successfully to pool the prices received from the two markets and to pay farmers at a rate which is an average of all receipts, although certain regional variations are allowed within the system. This is a legacy less of the 1930's than of the 1940's, when the government could allocate supplies more directly between markets and the Minister could fix prices for retail consumption at his own discretion, even though these powers were subsequently restricted.

Since 1934, however, the MMB's have enjoyed the authority to compel all milk to be sold through their agency. By this means they have been able to regulate the balance between liquid and manufacturing markets. The problems have been, and remain, difficult. In the early years the Board took it upon itself to promote the liquid milk market, achieved great success but subsequently saw the mountain begin to crumble. In the 1930's and again in the 1950's and 1960's the Boards also attempted to increase the domestic share of the trade in manufactured milk products, partly to absorb recurrent seasonal surpluses, but the competition from Commonwealth and EFTA suppliers in the 1960's was not only effective in respect of price and quality but also for long periods favoured by government. Nevertheless the Boards, sometimes on their own account, sometimes in collaboration with large manufacturers like Unilever, Associated Dairies, the CWS and numerous specialised creameries, generally succeeded in processing almost all the surpluses of raw milk in Britain. No stockpile of dehydrated or emulsified milk products existed before the UK joined the Common Market.

The MMB's have been fortunate in having a commodity that can be switched between two markets, but a monopsony over milk supplies is not in itself sufficient to ensure commercial success. Milk is a highly seasonal product. In November output reaches its low point. This is a fact of life that has been constant since at least the 1950's. The MMB's have therefore been compelled to make certain that supplies of liquid milk are sufficient to satisfy demand every autumn and especially in the weeks before Christmas. Winter milk supplies have been adequate in most years only to satisfy the liquid milk market.

Shortages cannot be made up be carrying stocks over from periods of abundance because the supply has been guaranteed for freshness ever since the 1930's. Technical developments — sterilisation, UHT processing and dehydration — could allow the Boards to place less emphasis on winter production, but popular taste has so far not encouraged the change. The surpluses at the height of the late spring flush are always too large for the liquid trade, but the MMB's have not been able to reduce the surplus by running down the size of the natural dairy herd, for fear of winter shortage. Thus whatever the state of competition from abroad, manufacturing has to be cherished in order to cope with the summer glut. Regulation of supply by staggering the time of calving, especially by encouraging autumn and winter calving, has been successful physiologically but its commercial results remain questionable. Dairy farmers obviously value the existence of a year-long market for their produce, but the costs to them, to the MMB's, and in government subsidies, of producing large quantities of winter milk are high, not least because most of their oversea competitors concentrate on processing the summer flush, when feed is cheap and contingent expenses at their least.

The MMB's are both extensive commercial organisations and regulatory agencies balancing complex market operations. They have almost become victims of their own success in the past decade or so. In co-operation with government the Boards, and their wartime surrogate, in 1940-54, turned Britain from a country with a relatively low *per capita* consumption of liquid milk in the 1930's to one with a high level of personal consumption by the end of the 1950's. Concentrated advertising played a part in this transformation, but the various publicly subsidised schemes such as the school milk allowance were probably more influential. Altogether, however, a subsidised retail price, fixed even after 1954 directly by the Ministry, combined with an efficient network of distribution operated in part by the Board and in part by commercial undertakings, guaranteed supplies to virtually every householder in the country. But whatever the cost, for farmers and for the MMB's the liquid milk trade was vital. Its relative decline in the past twenty years has begun to put economic pressure upon the Boards and their related commercial operations, not least upon the doorstep delivery service indirectly or directly controlled by the Boards since the late 1950's, and these strains may prove too forceful to resist in an era of vast EEC surpluses and rivalry, even in the liquid milk trade, from the near Continent. One particular difficulty has arisen with the growth of large supermarket chains which do not necessarily wish to accept the monopoly of the MMB's in the distribution of milk; alternative supplies of long-life milk, not yet a grave threat to pasteurised supplies, offer supermarkets and other retail outlets a potential lever to undermine the Boards' negotiating strength. On the other hand the Boards' functions have even expanded since Britain entered the EEC, for with the yearly growing stocks of dairy produce in intervention their role as public agencies of the dairy industry now includes responsibility for processing the unsalable but inexpendable produce of British cows' exuberance.

The Milk Marketing Boards have acquired a public reputation for reliability and commercial success. Since the 1950's they indeed have become more visible to the consumer, with their interest in retailing both liquid milk and dairy produce. The other Boards in agricultural marketing have either been unsuccessful or have concentrated on wholesale distribution, with virtually no public 'profile'. The small-scale success of the Hop Marketing Board, for example, has been repeated in the Wool Marketing Board, which was able to capture the lion's share of the wholesale market in a fairly homogeneous industrial raw material. The Board gained the confidence of the farmers who had wool to sell by obtaining reasonably good prices and establishing clearly understood standards of quality; and also of the woollen manufacturers, who had no objection to dealing direct with a centralised institution. The Board had been established in particular circumstances. In 1950 government decided to include wool among the commodities for which prices were guaranteed, but required an agency to bring growers and merchants together. The Wool Marketing Board was the result. The effect of the Board's intervention within a few years of its establishment was to stabilise prices and prevent broad seasonal fluctuations. The Board administered the prices guaranteed by government in the annual review but staggered payments throughout the year. Since all growers are required to be members of the scheme, the Board has distributed all the wool clipped each year and has succeeded in reducing the impact of international oscillations of price on British farmers so that the wild fluctuations of the 1930's have become a thing of the past. At its peak in the later 1960's the Board had 130,000 farmers under its control and disposed of more than 85 million lb of wool. At the same time it developed links, especially in publicity, with the International Wool Secretariat. The Board's chief difficulty, acute in the 1966–69 recession and unresolved in subsequent years of less depressed conditions of trade, was competition from man-made fibres. This had been a long-standing hazard, but until the later 1960's the Board had actually managed to improve the producers' prices for wool when the subsidy guaranteed by government was declining in real terms. It was the sudden cheapness and variety of artificial fibres that caused the downturn after 1966. On the other hand, sheep farmers no longer depend upon wool as a principal source of income. The rise in the numbers of sheep kept in Britain since 1970 owes nothing to wool prices, which have remained sticky for most of the period.

Horticulturists were also urged by government and the National Farmers' Union to take heed to the marketing of their produce. In the 1940's distributional schemes for several minor commodities that the government hoped to include among those with guaranteed prices were proposed, but only two emerged to be tested at the hands of the producers who could be corralled into a public body, and one, the proposed Apple and Pear Board, was defeated in a poll of producers, chiefly because the growers of apples for culinary and dessert purposes and growers of cider apples had little in common. The other, the Tomato and Cucumber Marketing Board, got off the ground but was beset with so many difficulties that the producer members eventually voted to abolish it. There were, in all the Boards during the 1950's and 1960's, abolitionists actively engaged in undermining their position; the horticultural marketing schemes seem to have been especially beleaguered by more independent spirits than the others.

On the other hand the stormiest history was that of the British Egg Marketing Board, because its commercial policies as much as its constitutional position were controversial. All the new Boards fashioned in the 1950's owed much to the potent advocacy of the NFU, whose heavy-handed corporatism alienated as many members as it prompted to envisage a future of agricultural stability and prosperity. The Egg Marketing Board was born in far from propitious circumstances even though the scheme, when placed before producers, was overwhelmingly accepted. There was uncertainty about its function. The Minister apparently believed that the Board would stabilise prices and thereby contain subsidies, the NFU that the subsidy proposed by government should be administered to the benefit of the farmers by a producer-controlled monopsony; others thought that the Board would so improve quality that there would be major advantages to the consumer. The result, however, was generally disappointing. The Board in effect continued the trading policies of the Ministry agency which preceded it in the egg business, so that it possessed no clear powers to raise prices for the producers nor authority to reduce the actual cost of support.

The BEMB began its operations in 1957 when *per capita* consumption was already high, by comparison with 1934, when the MMB's began their operations, and when the share of domestic consumption provided from farms at home exceeded 95 per cent. The manufacturing trade in eggs was small so that the tendency to surplus in production could not be absorbed by diverting supplies to it to the same extent as the MMB's were able to do. The guaranteed prices of the 1940's and the subsidies which followed in the 1950's were already encouraging farmers towards overproduction by 1957. Moreover the distribution network, especially the system of packing stations, inherited by the Board were not only expensive to maintain but tended to set the trade in too rigid a pattern, just at a time when commercial forces were beginning to alter the whole structure of the economy in ways that were difficult for the BEMB to control. The Board's problem was that it was required by law to receive all the eggs unloaded on it by producers but could not enforce restrictions of production

nor prevent farmers from dealing direct with consumers. Any attempt to interfere with this 'free' market was decried as unwarrantable interference by farmers who tended only to offer their unsalable surpluses to the Board for distribution. But if it could not control producers the BEMB could attempt at least to influence consumers.

In this, however, the Board signally failed. Attempting to emulate the MMBs' achievement — that is, standardise eggs on the market — it miscalculated public attitudes to quality. Eggs to be sold retail were stamped with the 'lion mark', intended to prevent double claims upon subsidies, which would also act as a guarantee of quality. But since collection and distribution in the 1960's were comparatively slow, the eggs were often far from fresh in the shops. By the late 1960's, indeed, some 40 per cent of all eggs produced in Britain did not pass through the BEMB: they drew no subsidy but, equally, paid no levies to the Board. In periods of glut many of these 'free' eggs were thrown on to the Board, which could only accept them and pay out the subsidy. To make matters worse the Board did not even reap the full benefits of an extensive promotion of eggs among consumers, because, although the 'message' got through, the public was often averse from lion-branded eggs. *Per capita* consumption increased by 15-20 per cent between 1957 and 1970 but the Board's problems accumulated. The attempt to reduce a large potential surplus in the late 1960's was expensive. Processing was encouraged to dispose of the superabundance, but this merely resulted in another surplus piling up in egg products. The chief stumbling block was that mass production was overtaking the egg trade just at the time when overproduction by traditional methods was also becoming significant. A plan to protect small producers in 1965 was a failure and added further acrimony to the Board's conduct of its business; but even if it had succeeded it would merely have enlarged the surplus. The Board was eventually would up in 1971 by the Minister's decision, to be replaced by a smaller supervisory body with few market functions, the Egg Authority.

The Potato Marketing Board continued its policy of the 1930's by avoiding direct involvement in trade through price fixing or price guarantees. Potatoes keep too well through the season to offer producers much natural protection. Orderly marketing is therefore difficult, partly because of potential competition from imports in times of scarcity and partly because yields are so variable from year to year and from region to region. On the other hand potatoes cannot be held over from one season to the next to equalise supplies. No guarantee scheme could rationally take account of these fluctuations without imposing restraints upon the acres planted with the crop. Quotas on acreage, and regulation of the size of potatoes put up for sale, have been the chosen instruments of control by the Board. Its attempt to control acreage was especially contentious in the 1950's and early 1960's, chiefly because it was held to restrain progressive farmers. On a rational analysis, however, the method worked successfully by keeping output and consumption more or less in line. But price fluctuations were still very marked, and farmers were aggrieved by recurrent seasons of low prices in the later 1960's and again in the later 1970's. Moreover the Board could do little to ameliorate the few seasons of acute shortage, such as 1962-63, when the weather was particularly adverse.

Marketing boards have proved a mixed success. One of their difficulties has been to develop a rational plan of economic management amid changes in both market opportunities and political attitudes. Before the war they operated in a more obviously voluntary manner, avoiding detailed political interference and encouraging co-operation. In the 1940's so many ideas of corporatist intervention floated in the air, being exhaled as much by the NFU as by government, that the functions of proposed marketing schemes were inevitably expressed in terms of control, regulation or induced efficiency. By contrast, in the 1950's even though the Conservative government instituted several marketing boards, enthusiasm for the notion of planning waned significantly. A revival of interest in the 1960's resulted in some new formulations in agricultural marketing, but economic circumstances were so different from those of the 1940's that the impetus for change was less marked. But the fusion of marketing schemes with the support system meant that, whatever political preferences governments expressed, the presence of the Ministry in setting prices or determining levels of subsidy was always more evident between the 1950's and 1970's than it had been in the 1930's. Thus even under the more liberal regime of Ministers of Agriculture between 1954 and 1964 the increasing anxiety of government not to retain 'open-ended' price guarantees and the inception of 'standard' quantities as a gauge for determining prices gave a new impulse to the Boards' longstanding attempts to restrict production through quotas. Predicting, or perhaps influencing, demand so as not to overproduce foodstuffs when government was reluctant to finance surpluses but unwilling to curtail imports became one of the chief preoccupations of marketing agencies in the 1950's and 1960's. That indeed may be taken as a measure of their success.

Two major agricultural commodities, grain and meat, were not subject to marketing schemes in the 1950's. It was believed to be too difficult to regulate the domestic trade in either, even though the ever-hopeful NFU had made comprehensive proposals in the 1940's and early 1950's for setting up producer-dominated agencies for both cereals and meat and livestock. In meat products the Pig and Bacon Marketing Board of the 1930's was a failure and was not revived after the war. No other attempt at an orthodox marketing board has been made. The NFU was thwarted in its efforts to institute a public agency in 1953, owing to strenuous opposition from the butchers and auctioneers. Subsidies payable upon fat livestock could be given either to the farmer or to the wholesaler of carcase meat and were administered direct by agents of the Ministry, so that the pattern of marketing remained flexible. On the other hand the auction mart did not necessarily serve the farmers' best interests, not least because slaughtering and meat wholesaling had increasingly fallen under the domination of large commercial concerns whose actions in the market could influence prices significantly. Middlemen and processors were well protected through mass organisation or the existence of trade associations. Farmers were not always even the chief beneficiaries of the system of price support.

The NFU therefore established a co-operative, the Fatstock Marketing Corporation (FMC), to oversee the trade and stabilise prices for its members. The FMC bought fatstock from any farmer and paid for the beef, lamb, pork or poultry meat on the *deadweight* value of the carcase, thus eliminating the skilful guesswork of the butcher in assessing livestock values, which, farmers believed, was employed against their interests, since judge and buyer were one and the same. The co-operative began with a capital of £10,000 but in its first year handled fatstock worth £100 million. Shortage of capital for development was a major difficulty, and in 1960 the status of the business was changed to that of a public company. Thereafter for about twenty years it flourished. At its zenith in the early 1970's the FMC handled half the bacon pigs, a quarter of the porkers and about 12-15 per cent of the cattle and sheep slaughtered in the UK. It moved successfully into the expanding poultry trade, not only buying turkey and broiler meat but processing much of the produce into attractive consumer packages; eventually the FMC became a large-scale primary producer of poultry meat. The Corporation has owned 120 slaughterhouses and employed over 11,000 people, many engaged in manufacturing meat products. By 1970 it was the largest meat-handling organisation in Europe, with important sidelines such as dressing hides and woolfells. Yet its financial course has been erratic. By the early 1980's it was on the point of collapse. The reasons for this sudden deterioration are complex, but misjudgement seems to have played an important part. The notoriously unstable bacon market, for example, was captured just at the time when a decline in consumption and vigorous oversea competition undermined the profitability of the trade. In the same way the FMC's large interest in poultry-dressing was not so dominant as to prevent the faster growth of competitors at home or the steady infiltration of markets from abroad. Altogether the aim of stabilising producers' prices was too difficult to achieve after 1975, and the Corporation laid out too much on processing on the principle that fresh meat surpluses had to be absorbed in order to hold farmers' prices up.

For cereals the pattern of marketing caused less distress to farmers than to the Ministry in the 1950's, for the system of deficiency payments was a constant drain on the Treasury until after 1962. In 1965, however, the government set up the Home Grown Cereals Authority. This was not a trading organisation. The Authority did, however, introduce a scheme to offer forward contract bonuses to encourage farmers to store grain in order to bring it to market in an orderly fashion. By 1970 about one-third of wheat and barley was already disposed of through this scheme, which was paid for half by Treasury grant and half by drawbacks upon the farmers' subsidies. Even so, the HGCA was concerned far more in work related to research and the collection of information; its chief success has been to bring together agricultural, commercial and academic experts in specialist committees. In this it resembles several similar commissions or associations sponsored by government — the Egg Authority, the Pig Industry Development Board, the Meat and Livestock Commission, of which only the last had real powers to regulate, but not to engage in, trade and to administer the subsidies paid by the Ministry. None was successful in commercial operations, but all did useful work in co-ordinating research and advisory publicity.

The most complex monopoly in agricultural marketing was excercised by the British Sugar Corporation during the forty-five years in which it existed as a quasi-public authority. The BSC was founded in 1936 at the time when sugar beet growing was beginning to expand beyond East Anglia. It was authorised to regulate production of home-grown sugar by purchasing all the beet grown, for processing in its factories. The BSC's control over production was monopolistic. It fixed quotas and, for much of the period, distributed seed. In addition, although the Corporation guaranteed to purchase authorised production, it acted as judge of both quality and price and regulated the throughput of its beet factories by licensing deliveries during each year's campaign. Its monopoly was restrained only by the fact of large cane-sugar imports. The government, indeed, found its double-headed commitment to domestic production and the protection of Commonwealth supplies distinctly uncomfortable in the 1950's. In 1956 the Sugar Board was set up to square the circle. The Board administered the complicated agreement to purchase Commonwealth sugar ratified in 1951 so as to sell it commercially, and also underpinned the BSC by enabling it to honour guarantees to British farmers, underwriting any deficit (or receiving any surplus) upon the Corporation's accounts. Sugar was unique, not only in the degree of its monopolisation but also in the fact that government was determined to maintain a strategic reserve of home produce almost irrespective of cost.

Several agricultural commodities were not subject to public marketing schemes, and many minor crops were not even considered in proposals for regulating trade. In a few instances the crops were so specialised that they were grown on contract to wholesalers or processors. This aspect of agricultural marketing is important, however, since it often challenges the pre-war (and post-war) assumption that primary producers were consistently in an uncompetitive position *vis-à-vis* the merchants and manufacturers. Growing primary products under contract in which the price was pre-arranged was a widespread practice after the war and has increased in the period since 1960. The system never encompassed more than a minority of farmers, and those who benefited were nearly always from among the well-to-do and enterprising. But it is worth recording that the essential feature of these arrangements is the need of processing firms to guarantee supplies of raw materials for their manufacturing. Thus bakers of crispbread have to ensure stocks of rye, not all of which is imported, but British farmers will grow the crop only if they can be certain of sales, since general demand is so slight. To a limited extent, also, oats and malting barleys are produced under contract for manufacturers. The most important of these arrangements, however, relate to vegetables, peas and green beans specially grown for freezing. Pea-vining is a major enterprise in East Anglia. Not only are the crops grown under contract but most of the field work is controlled by the processing companies, for whom both culture and harvesting are critical. The evidence is unclear, but it appears likely that contract growing is a commoner solution to the food processors' problems of supply than the purchase and direct exploitation of land by manufacturing enterprises on their own account. It has not been uncommon, however, for farmers or farming companies to build and operate their own processing plants in freezing, freeze drying, grass drying, no less than in traditional manufacturing such as cider-making or butchery and milk processing.

6 · Prices, productivity and investment

Price currents

Since the war agricultural prices have increased at less than the rate of inflation generally. By comparison with the mid-1950's they averaged about 80 in terms of the retail all-price index, with a range for individual commodities between 60 and 85 at the end of the 1970's. Actual prices, of course, have risen, and in some years, as in the late 1960's and after 1972, the increase in money terms was substantial. There is some evidence to suggest that agricultural prices, especially food prices, may have led other prices upwards for a few years after the world-wide dearth in 1972, although the picture is confused by the effect of other influences, the oil crisis and the pressure of higher wage demands. In any event the 1970's witnessed a major upward revision of all farm prices. Thus between 1971-73 and 1981-82 agricultural prices rose by 200 per cent. Coming after a long period of modest inflation of agricultural prices this upward trend was disconcerting. Its causes were much debated, especially by players in the Common Market game, but the outcome, despite several shocks to the system, was not a trend in farm prices outrunning other movements in a severely inflationary period. Nevertheless the debate did produce some reflections upon long-run price trends in agriculture which require consideration.

There are differences in price trends for particular commodities and between product and input prices, but the general indices do reflect underlying movements. No unbroken series exists for the whole period from the 1930's to the 1980's, but it is possible to see the pattern quite clearly even from discontinous indices. The indices reveal three distinctive periods in which price currents set and then changed direction. First, the second world war, post-war austerity and the shock caused by the Korean War, from 1939 to 1953, saw prices rise threefold.

This increase was obviously induced in part by government intervention, but it would have taken place in some form without central planning because the shortages caused by the war and post-war dislocation altered the terms of trade for primary products and transformed the bargaining position of agriculturists by comparison with the inter-war years. The rate of inflation in the 1940's was higher than supply conditions portended also because prices ruling in the base years of the index, 1936–38, were low and because notably increased purchasing power, with the return of full employment after 1940, instigated at least latent demand-pull inflation. Had shortages persisted beyond the early 1950's, as many experts predicted, this demand-led inflation, suppressed or restrained by controls upon supply until 1949-54, would have had a serious effect on price trends in the next phase. However, from about 1953 more or less continuously until the harvest of 1972 real farm prices remained stable. Indeed, the inclination of the trend before 1970 was downward. There were years in which real prices rose quite sharply, but they were latter-day instances of the immemorial problems caused to farmers and their customers by seasonal dearth. Such bad years were not numerous in the age of plenty, at least for well-to-do Western consumers, but events such as the savage winter of 1962-63 did leave their mark on annual price movements. Poor harvests, affecting a variety of commodities over much of the world's agricultural land, became more frequent in the early and mid-1970's. Shortages were acute in 1972-73 and expectations were gloomy. In Europe the dry seasons of 1975–76 also reduced output and forced prices up. Coupled with the other factors which fostered inflation, the brief but disconcerting episode of renewed scarcity brought about another change of trend in agricultural prices. Coinciding with the period of transition for the United Kingdom in coming to terms with life under the EEC Common Agricultural Policy was a threefold rate of agricultural price inflation which effectively destroyed the basis of long-run stability achieved in the previous decades of price subsidisation. Without the upward trend in the 1970's the secular decline of prices for agricultural commodities would have been very considerable.

International conditions of supply have influenced economists in predicting trends in the terms of trade which in turn have formed a main element in political decision-making. However responsive politicians have been to the aspirations of farmers since the 1940's, their policies have inevitably been shaped by wider economic conditions than the issue of agricultural well-being. High price levels might be justified as a necessary charge upon the economy when the overriding need was to ensure supplies and the prognosis was despondent, or they might be justified as a social instrument to maintain stability and a desired relationship between producers' incomes and consumers' expenditure, but prices above prevailing international levels could not be defended in the same terms throughout the post-war period. The international terms of trade, which in the 1940's and early 1950's were inclined to favour primary producers owing to the dislocations caused by the war and reconstruction, swung over to the benefit of manufacturing exporters later in the 1950's. Whereas, in an earlier period of large-scale movement in favour of industrial production from 1875 to 1910, the principal cause of the swing against primary production was the extension of production, the adverse trend after 1953 was brought about by improved productivity as much as by territorial expansion. Accordingly the effects upon farm incomes have been less severe than in the late nineteenth century, even though a direct comparison is impossible owing to the much greater incidence of subsidisation since 1950.

However, expert opinion in the 1940's led politicians to expect a long period of comparative food shortage even after the war was over. Colin Clark, for example, predicted that in 1960 primary products would have doubled in price in relation to manufactured goods by comparison with 1935–38. Not only the shortages directly attributable to the war but also trends in technological development bearing upon manufacturing were thought to be conclusive. No one foresaw the exponential growth of agriculture in the 1950's and 1960's, but everyone was very conscious of the under-performance of industry in the inter-war years and its virtually inevitable rebound under wartime and post-war planning. Government could not accept all the implications of *carte blanche* support for agricultural expansion, if only because the Treasury could not find the money, but it is striking that few politicians, administrators or economists seriously questioned the *idea* of maximum production at all costs until after 1947 and the Cripps economy drive.

The problem in the period of scarcity was to find a reference price of each agricultural commodity that would not over-stretch the financial resources of the Ministry, that would be acceptable to farmers, whose co-operation and general prosperity the government hoped to secure, and that would not deter consumers and encourage the black market. At a time of acute shortages when almost all food products can be sold without promotion (*pace* whale meat, snoek and ground-nut oil) price in theory hardly matters. Governments, however, were set upon improving diets and upon the more equitable distribution of what was available, and since they handled all but a tiny fraction of the agricultural commodities on sale there was no need to ration by price. Moreover it was not necessary to maintain any close relationship between producers' prices and consumers' prices. Farmers were paid an incentive price for produce that was required, but output could also be controlled by quotas and improvement grants. The prices agreed usually bore some relationship to international prices, if only because in most sections of agriculture the UK was still heavily dependent upon imports to make up short supplies and food processors had to be sure of comparable prices for home-produced and imported ingredients.

There is no simple correlation between price trends and the action of government intervention and corporate monopsony. Price controls were systematically reduced in the early 1950's until only milk remained as a commodity regulated directly by the Minister. Hops, wool and sugar beet, however, have been controlled in price more or less continuously since the war, even though not all the marketing boards were able to stabilise prices for the products they managed. It is true that, with the possible exception of hops and milk, oligopolists in Britain could not disregard international price movements in fixing British prices. It had not been possible even in the late 1940's, when the United Kingdom had something like a siege economy, to regulate prices without reference to the North

American market from which much of the deficiency in home supplies was made up. The tendency in the 1940's was for world prices to rise as the terms of trade moved against the consumers of food. Thus, whereas wheat prices on the Chicago exchange at least doubled between 1936-38 and 1947-49, the increase in Britain approached threefold (7s 9d per cwt in 1936-38 and 20s 4d in 1947-49). A similar trend in which world prices rose but fell behind the increase of Britain wholesale prices was seen in sugar, wool, butter and beef, although in the last instance the price movement was distorted by dislocation of the Argentinian trade. The government, needing to acquire imports of many temperate foodstuffs, was faced with a choice between reducing supplies available for home consumption and paying international contract prices and fixing producer prices at home accordingly so as not to deter domestic production. In practice the choice was less stark; some imports continued to be bought, and farmers at home were offered incentive prices in the hope that they would increase output in order to reduce dependence upon imports.

Considered in the longer term, the difference of trend between regulated prices and market prices when the latter were allowed to find a level without direct intervention was not wide. Thus wheat prices fell by about 5 per cent between 1955-57 and 1965-67, wool by about 7 per cent and eggs by about a third, whereas all carcase meat prices rose, by over 20 per cent in the case of beef and by 15 per cent for pork; potatoes increased by about 17 per cent and beet sugar by 15 per cent, all in real terms. Milk, which was controlled in price throughout, rose by about 5 per cent between 1955-57 and 1965-67. In other words there is no clear correlation between intervention and price movements. This point was clearly understood by government, since the concept of deficienacy payments depends for its justification upon the belief that direct control in order to achieve or maintain optimal prices was unworkable as well as distasteful to government in the mid-1950's. Farmers were protected by 'topping up' the sums they received for their commodities in the market place.

Price, in the silver age of British agricultural policy during the 1950's and 1960's, may not have been significantly influenced by intervention, but it would be unreal to consider the effect of price currents upon agricultural prosperity without reference to the volume of price subsidies. At its peak in the early 1960's the system of price guarantees cost £200 millions a year: The heavy expenditure of 1961-62 was hardly planned and led to a sharp reaction in government. Thereafter the cost of subsidies was reduced, partly by changing the levels of support but chiefly through the system of 'standard quantities' which fixed a maximum quota of production to qualify for subsidy. By the end of the 1960's the annual cost of price supports was about £180 million a year at current prices, rather less in real terms than in the late 1950's. Indeed, the guaranteed prices in 1971 and 1972 for many commodities were little different from those paid after the harvests of 1957 and 1958, despite an inflation of about 50 per cent: wheat, 1957, £1·42 per cwt, 1971, £1·63; barley, £1·45 and £1·45 respectively; fat cattle, £13·05 per cwt gross and £13·20 per cwt gross; sugar beet, £6·53 per ton in 1957 and £7·60 in 1971. Some support prices, however, had notably increased — potatoes from £11·25 to £16·55 per ton and sheep meat from 16·4p per lb to 24·3p. Some guarantees, e.g. for milk and eggs, were actually less in 1971 than in 1957.

The relative importance of guarantees declined with the accelerated inflation of the late 1960's and early 1970's. Until 1972 the real price of most farm produce was declining in relation to the retail price index. Accordingly the burden of price supports should have risen in order to maintain producers' prices. It was not necessary to increase them, thanks to the effectiveness of rising productivity, although the farmers

The cost of price subsidisation in the early 1960's (£ million)

Commodity	1959-60	1960-61	1961-62	1962-63	1964-65
(a) Cereals	58·4	63·4	73·3	63·7	77·0
(b) Potatoes	1·0	5·7	8·0	0·4	0·5
(c) Eggs	33·1	22·5	16·2	21·5	21·0
(d) Fatstock	50·9	46·2	113·3	101·1	87·7
(e) Milk (except welfare milk)	8·5	10·8	11·8	nil	nil
(f) Wool	2·8	2·6	2·9	3·2	0·6
(Current prices)	154·7	151·2	225·5	190·1	186·8

did not always see the changes of policy in this light. In terms of gross output price support accounted for about 15 per cent in the years between 1958 and 1963, but only about 9 per cent in 1969-71. More specifically, deficiency payments for cereals at the flood of the tide averaged about one-third of market value. The subsidy on fat cattle varied between 9 and 26 per cent of market value, whereas that for milk did not exceed 0·4 per cent of the retail price. In 1969-71 the corresponding figures were less — cereals 15-20 per cent, fat cattle 12 per cent, etc. The prospect of eventual membership of the EEC influenced policy objectives in the government, particularly after 1970. As the CAP practice of inducing prices to rise to remunerative levels was adopted the part played by price guarantees obviously changed. Subsidies to farmers have continued. Indeed, the cost to the Exchequer of paying for producers' intervention sales and of keeping surpluses in store has become burdensome. Subsidies other than capital grants (a larger measure than price guarantees) fell from about 12 per cent of total receipts in agriculture in 1969-71 to 6 per cent in 1977-78 but thereafter began to rise again. Much of the support offered in the 1970's was in the form of production grants rather than price guarantees, but the ratio was variable. Thus in 1974-75 cattle price subsidies amounted to £63·7 million whereas production grants totalled £106·5 million; in 1975-76, £113 million and £88·3 million respectively; and in 1976-77 £16·3 million and £102·7 million. In 1974-75 price subsidies altogether were £134·9 million and in 1980-81 £167·3 million. Intervention service costs rose by about 275 per cent in the same period. Several commodities — pig meat, poultry, eggs, wool — were not, or were very little, subsidised under CAP rules. Production grants were preferred as a means of supporting all but the main products, so that the burden of subvention fell very unequally upon the Commission and affected agricultural development in a rather distorted fashion.

Rising living standards bring about improvements in human diet. This tendency is not infinite, however, and for most commodities there seems to be optimum level of *per capita* comsumption beyond which the principle of diminishing returns comes into action. In the case of eggs the pattern is very clear. In the ten years after 1954 *per capita* consumption of eggs in shell increased from below 150 to about 200 per annum. In the past fifteen years consumption has fluctuated but never increased beyond the limit reached the mid-1960's, even in favourable years. Yet price elasticity has continued to fall more or less steadily since the mid-1950's. In the years of expanding consumption price elasticity at least halved, but it also halved again in the subsequent period of stagnant consumption. Moreover the first phase more or less coincided with a period of productivity gain almost equal to the rise in *per capita* consumption. There was then a small but useful opportunity to increase gross output by keeping greater numbers of egg-laying birds, but with both static consumption and a slowing down in the rate of population growth since 1970 the downward trend of real prices seems to have been the result of competition in the market for eggs. The problems of the egg industry in the 1970's have been compounded if not solely caused by the stickiness of demand. The optimum consumption of about 200 *per capita* per annum cannot easily be raised, certainly not in the long term, but, equally, in conditions of general personal affluence demand has not significantly fallen from the plateau thus reached. There may be pressures upon particular commodities, not induced by effective purchasing power: eggs have suffered slightly from the competition of other protein foods since the 1970's and from fashions in personal health, notably the widely publicised fears about cholesterol.

For almost every kind of agricultural produce price elasticity in Britain declined between the 1950's and the 1970's. In many cases the fall has exceeded 50 per cent, and for all but certain meat products and fresh vegetables the ratios of price elasticity of demand were below 1·00 by the 1970's. Real prices have fallen as personal disposable incomes have risen. The price fall is partly attributable to long-run reductions in the world prices of traded commodities since the end of the Korean War and partly, probably more significantly, to increments of productivity. Those commodities which have showed the largest gains in productivity have fallen furthest in real price. Nevertheless this correlation is modified by patterns of demand. There is no clear evidence that demand for

99

agricultural produce has become sated in the way that consumption of milk and eggs has levelled off in the past fifteen years. However, although to some extent it can be predicted and formed through publicity campaigns, demand has not been effectively controlled by food producers, who have often been surprised by the trends that have set in throughout western Europe.

One of the most interesting changes relates to cheese. Meat consumption in Britain has changed much since the war. Poultry meat and pork, the production of which has become highly intensive if not industrialised, have become more popular, while demand for beef, bacon and lamb has declined. All meat products have fallen in price in real terms, but the price of poultry and pork has declined more than the price of beef. This presumably explains the differential pattern of consumption. Yet the simple equation of rising consumption and falling prices does not apply to cheese. Cheese consumption has risen steadily since the mid-1950's. By 1975-80 demand for the product was one-third to two-fifths greater than in 1953-56. Cheese prices, however, have fallen less in real terms than those of any other agricultural product, except lamb; indeed, in the early 1980's they were approximately equal to the prices ruling after the end of food control. No one can explain this trend convincingly, but one element in the formation of personal taste must have been the greatly increased range of choice available. The dairy industry certainly gained from the growing demand for cheese, which was especially active in the period when consumption of liquid milk was receding, but the chief beneficiaries have been oversea suppliers, since 1973 particularly from other Common Market countries.

Butter consumption, however, has followed a different course from that of cheese. The taste for butter increased steadily during the 1950's and into the 1960's. The reaction against rationing and scarcity was a strong pent-up demand which was satisfied in the following ten years. Most of it was met by imports, especially from Australasia. So plentiful were supplies by the early 1960's that prices had fallen accordingly and consumption *per capita* was approaching its peak. Between 1955-56 and 1965-66 individual consumption increased from 15 lb to 20 lb a year; thereafter a decline set in, until by the early 1980's consumption had fallen back to the level of the mid-1950's. Undoubtedly the upward pressure on prices in the 1970's, chiefly to bring the level in Britain closer to the prices prevailing in the EEC, was a major deterrent to consumption. The association in British demand schedules of butter with bread may have played a part also, since bread consumption fell significantly in the 1960's and 1970's. Furthermore butter suffered from competition with margarines, particularly in the period beginning in the late 1960's, when the 'image' of margarine and its palatability were much improved. Eventually the pendulum swung even further, because the newer vegetable oil margarines were promoted on grounds of health at the expense of butter, which, like cream, eggs and certain meats was castigated for containing too much saturated fat and cholesterol.

'Faddism' has become an independent variable in determining demand for foodstuffs. it is, of course, an inevitable consequence of affluence coupled with extensive publicity. As such it fits the conceptual framework constructed by theorists of demand, who have long accepted that consumption of particular commodities tends to become volatile when primary demand has been satisfied. This volatility is only partly price-determined, even though price may often become more significant when people can afford a wide range of primary products than it is when demand is focused upon a few staples. Agriculture has not only achieved abundance since the war, it has put on the market such a variety of commodities that choice has become distended. More generally it is probable that demand will reach an optimal level, a plateau of consumption perhaps inclined downwards, for virtually all temperate foods once general affluence has become established, since there is apparently a limit to the amount laid out in the household budgets upon food, regardless of the switching between commodities which takes place. In the past this *terminus ad quem* did not impend too closely upon agricultural production plans, because many households were still rising in the scale of affluence and because of continuing demographic expansion. Population growth has recently become attenuated, and the potential for new demand created by the formation of new households throughout the Common Market is now much diminished.

To the question of rising living standards the response is less clear, since the process of enrichment still has far to go, but the easy gains have been made, and the combination of substantial long-run unemployment and chronic poverty offers little prospect of a massive expansion in demand for agricultural produce. With higher food prices induced by EEC policy, the elasticity of demand for foods has regressed since the mid-1970's among the lower two quintiles of the population. It is a pattern in miniature of the plight affecting world trade in food, where large numbers can neither produce enough for self-sufficiency nor afford to buy the surpluses piling up in the developed temperate lands. On the face of it, both supply and effective demand should have caused a major recession of agricultural prices by the 1970's. The comparatively modest fall in real prices for food, mentioned above, has been buoyed up by government intervention and the lingering influence of monopolies. The distortion is especially marked in the price history of certain commodities. Thus butter and sugar both became relatively dear at a time when the underlying trend of consumption was downward, and bread, which for most of the past thirty years has suffered from the revulsion of public taste against carbohydrates, by a skilful indirect manipulation of its retail price has hardly declined in real terms since the war.

One would expect of commodities with low and declining price elasticity — which means nearly all the staple products of British agriculture — that fluctuations in supply would lead to substantial oscillations of price. For many commodities, e.g. pork, eggs and potatoes, this has been the case since 1960, but for some, above all for milk, in which seasonal output fluctuates widely, price control or monopsony has smoothed all such oscillations at retail level. General price stability, however, has been greater than the ratios of price elasticity would suggest, chiefly because, since the 1960's at least, there has been a potential surplus of supply over consumption at most periods; even the decline in dependence upon imported foods has not significantly altered the underlying stability of price trends, since it has affected neither the pattern of distribution nor the holding of stocks. There have inevitably been organisational changes tending to maintain this stability. Consolidation of holdings on the one hand and the parallel movement towards large-scale manufacturing and distribution of primary produce on the other hand have absorbed many of the shocks caused by price fluctuations and long-run changes in demand.

Output and productivity

Gross output of agriculture has increased since the late 1930's by about 2·3 per cent per annum, achieved during a period when numbers employed in the industry have fallen drastically and the area of agricultural land available for use has also contracted. The yield of arable land may have risen by well over 80 per cent since 1940 and of grass land by half or more. This rate of increase was three or perhaps four times greater than the gains in productivity made during the first forty years of the century. The United Kingdom reduced its dependence upon imported foodstuffs between 1935 and 1965 by almost half, and the trend has continued in the past fifteen years despite market penetration by Continental food producers within the Common Market free trade area. By the late 1970's Britain had once again become a net exporter of some agricultural produce. Domestic agriculture has not only been able to satisfy a larger proportion of home demand but has adapted quite successfully to changes of preference in British demand schedules. The shifting balance between arable and pastoral shows this versatility clearly, although the subtler changes in crop preferences or patterns of stock-keeping are more conclusive. British agriculture is limited by climate and geology. Within these constraints, however, output has expanded in unprecedented fashion. Much of the old diversity, the vernacular stamp of agriculture, has been sacrificed for standardised procedures seen to produce the best results, but in truth one form of diversity has been replaced by another, since specialisation has turned out to be one of the most telling influences upon efficiency. Efficiency and high productivity may not be synonymous, but the efforts of agriculturists and the majority of their advisers since the war have turned upon the achievement of both simultaneously.

Common opinion that agriculture has been one of the most successful sectors of the economy since 1940 is justified by the evidence of rising output and expanding productivity. Agriculture stands high in terms of net factor productivity, that is to say, the quotient of net output divided by primary-source inputs. It has been making steady progress in this respect since the 1950's, but aided, as we shall see, by the comparatively poor performance of many other sectors. From once being regarded as an industry with an irreversibly low level of productivity, farming could easily stand comparison with both manufacturing and services by the 1970's.

The most striking evidence of increased efficiency comes from the data of labour productivity. Since about 1950 the annual improvement in labour productivity has averaged about 6 per cent, by comparison with less than 3 per cent for the whole economy. Moreover until very recent years the trend has been accelerating, from about 4 per cent before 1955, 5 per cent in the later 1950's and 6 per cent in the 1960's to reach 7 per cent for several years around 1970. This is impressive, but the rate of improvement has corresponded with that of other developed agricultural countries, although in the case of some, such as France and Italy, the base upon which the expansion has been founded was very low at the end of the war. Throughout the 1950's and 1960's labour productivity in agriculture in western Europe, in the United States, Canada and Australasia was rising at rates between 3 and 6 per cent. What stands out in Britain is the much better performance of agriculture by comparison with all other sectors except oil refining, chemicals, gas and electricity generation. Nevertheless no sector outdid agriculture between 1954 and 1973, and some, such as food processing and distribution, which were very profitable, showed quite poor rates of improvement in labour productivity.

Labour productivity is a useful measure of relative efficiency but it can obviously be misleading. If total output is stagnant or falling at the same time as the work force is being reduced, significant gains in productivity will be recorded, as the recession of 1979-83 clearly indicates. In the case of agriculture, output has grown at about the same rate as productivity has improved in the whole economy, while labour has declined to

Expenditure, general cropping farms (£ per farm)

	1961	1980
Labour	2,679	14,145
Feed	1,226	8,496
Fertilisers	852	6,793
Machinery	2,044	18,198
Total inputs	9,568	64,293

fewer than half the numbers employed in 1945-50. But this has brought about a large switch of resources to capital goods, machinery, fertilisers, concentrated feeding-stuffs, pesticides, all of which have resulted in labour saving as much as they have raised the volume of production. The transfer of resources from labour- to capital-intensive modes of production in terms of physical output is inherently more efficient.

Whether the change has produced an equal increase in the return upon investment is less certain, for the *cost* of achieving high physical and high labour productivity may have been excessive. Everything depends upon the use to which the gains in output are applied. The Farm Management Survey indicates the declining proportion of the farmers' outgoings devoted to labour and the corresponding rise in the amount spent upon machinery, fertilisers, feedstuffs and the like, as the accompanying table shows. More widely, labour inputs averaged 43 per cent in 1946, 24 per cent in 1956 but only about 20 per cent after 1965. Few people questioned this trend, unless on aesthetic grounds, before 1973 and the energy crisis. High farming had always implied heavy expenditure on purchased inputs in order to enlarge production. Practice did not always support theory, but the general view, inherited from the nineteenth century and refined through countless scientific experiments and field trials, was that the costs of improvement were justified by increasing returns. The backsliding that occurred between 1880 and the 1930's seemed to confirm progressive prejudices in favour of capital intensity, if only because the 'dog and stick' approach, while it may have minimised losses in hard times, did not give a profitable living.

Future success, as almost everyone believed in the 1930's and 1940's, lay in raising the fertility of the soil, in increasing stocking densities, in extracting more milk, eggs, lean meat, grass and grass crops, together with anything else that could be profitably cultivated from British holdings, at a cost that would not deter consumers nor overburden government. The outcome was impressive. Yields which had formerly increased but slowly were transformed in the 1950's and 1960's. In the long view the improvement of physical productivity after the war has been unprecedented. In the past there had always been some contraint upon rising productivity according to the intrinsic quality of the soil. Thus in periods of falling demand for grain, as after 1875, the contraction of the area under cereals helped to maintain average yields whatever the conditions of cultivation, because the least suitable arable fell out of tillage for the most part, leaving only good corn land still in crops. Conversely the massive expansion in the acreage sown to grain after about 1770 had caused much unfit, even sub-marginal, arable to be pressed into service, with a consequent drawback upon yields. There was a considerable increase of yields in the early nineteenth century, however, because of the progress made in improving cultivations. Broadly speaking, yields of wheat and barley rather more than doubled between 1700 and 1850. In 1885-89, when statistics of annual average yields were first collected officially, wheat produced about 16 cwt per acre in Great Britain and barley 15·5 cwt per acre. In 1945-49 the averages were 19 and 18, and from that period improvement was more persistent:

	1955-59	1965-69	1972-76	1980-81
Wheat	25	32	34	46.5
Barley	24	30	30	35

Comparable improvements occurred in most other commodities, although it is not possible to measure increments of yield in the case of several, such as beef, lamb and pork, since alterations in consumer preferences and in breeding and feeding practices have brought about widespread qualitative rather than quantitatiye changes. But for milk, potatoes, sugar beet and eggs physical improvements are measurable. Thus the yield of milk from cows increased from

540 gallons a year in 1940 to 608 gallons in 1955 and 632 gallons in 1965. For specifically dairy cows yields rose from 691 gallons in 1955 to 808 in 1965 and over 1,000 gallons by 1980. The two series are not compatible, but we can presume a rate of increase of at least 67 per cent between 1940 and 1980, which is much greater than in any earlier generation. The yield of eggs per bird also increased by between one-half and two-thirds between the 1940's and the 1970's, but from a comparatively low base of 130-150 a year until the 1950's. Sugar beet was producing about eight tons per acre in the later 1920's and about ten tons in the late 1940's. Yields had risen only to thirteen tons in 1965-76 and fourteen tons in 1980-81. Potatoes increased in about the same proportion, from seven tons in the late 1940's to about twelve tons in the 1970's. Except for wheat and barley, therefore, agricultural yields, in terms of physical quantities, have not doubled since the war, even though the rate of improvement has everywhere been outstanding. We should always bear in mind, however, that early in the twentieth century yields were already high by international standards; only a small number of agricultural economies could equal the productivity of the soil in Great Britain even in the 1920's and 1930's.

The coincidence of improved yields with the application of new scientific techniques is conspicuous. New strains of seed, varieties selected for their capacity to produce high yields, especially when combined with resistance to disease, together with new techniques of animal breeding, both the choice of progeny and nurture, may be regarded as crucial. Placing virtually the whole emphasis upon functional attributes immediately desired is a characteristic of post-war breeding technology. In plant breeding strains are selected that will produce the maximum yield, and secondary characteristics, apart from resistance to disease, are disregarded.

No importance is attached to the straw, since so much of it is destined to be burnt in the field, because in combine-harvesting negligible straw, capable only of holding up the ears in rain or after heavy application of nitrogenous fertilisers, is what is desired. In wheat the soft-milling varieties, well suited both to the British climate and British techniques of cultivation, have been most successful; the

107

commonest varieties grown since the 1950's, which have changed from time to time, have all been of this type. In barley breeding rather more emphasis has been placed upon feeding varieties rather than malting varieties. Maltsters have made the best of this, since in good years many strains of feed barley are suitable for malting. These points of emphasis are understandable. At least until the later 1970's, bread-making was dependent upon imported North American grain, with which British producers could not compete for quality. In the same way the greatest increase in demand for barley came from animal husbandry, not malting, so the plant breeders concentrated on the varieties for which they could expect the most extensive application.

Animal breeding followed a rather similar course, with emphasis upon those stocks which could satisfy the most specialised systems of production. Thus dairy cows were increasingly restricted as to breed types. The Friesian, and to a less extent its close congener, the Holstein, dominated the commercial dairy herds after the 1950's, replacing other breeds such as the Dairy Shorthorn or the Ayrshire and supplanting most dual-purpose beasts in dairy herds. Improvements in breeds could be achieved only in part by scientific research; straightforward breed selection and progeny testing, especially by means of the national scheme of artificial insemination, played a larger role. In the case of other livestock, breeding or managerial improvements were also more important in practice than genetic experiments. Men were able to get more out of their herds and flocks by selection of progeny and by nurture of the young — maximising the natural prolificity of the animals, in other words, and reducing the risk of postnatal casualty.

But breeding was not the only 'scientific' contibution to the improvement of yields. New feeding-stuffs and with them the concept of balanced rations, new kinds of fertilisers and pesticides, mechanisation of agricultural operations throughout the industry, better techniques of animal husbandry and cultivation owed much to the application of scientific innovations. Many came out of pragmatic observation or from field trials, conducted often by commercial enterprises, but, in terms of productivity, progress since the war can be attributed to a scientific revolution, infused by the capacity of agriculture to pay for a wide range of innovations and by the willingness of progressive farmers to adopt them.

In recent years the question of relative productivity has shifted ground, from the simple comparison of physical quantities or of output in relation to labour to an assessment of the comparative overall costs of achieving a unit of output. Efficiency is the measure of the use of capital and labour. A large application of capital, or a high volume of inputs, may not produce a return in yields able to stand comparison with less expensive modes of production in different agricultural systems. But even this consideration is open to dispute, since the balance between labour costs and investment is critical; in other words, it is seldom possible to substitute capital intensity for labour intensity without contingent changes in other areas. Moreover exchange rates, internal price levels and the differences between full-time and part-time employment in agriculture complicate the issues. Thus comparisons of output in terms of costs priced in different currencies produce rather variable results. In a table of productivity rankings evaluated under the various price systems of the UK, the Netherlands and France in the mid-1970's, the position of the United Kingdom ranged from fourth out of eight to sixth; it was beaten in all by Belgium-Luxembourg, the Netherlands and Denmark. It is, however, obviously of some advantage for all but the best performers to have the assessment calculated in terms of one's own prices, which indicates that agricultural regimes have an internal dynamic owing more to traditional expectations than to a conscious striving for efficiency of resource use. The calculations are based on relative, not absolute quantities. The comparatively poor performance of the UK is apparently accounted for by the high level of inputs, since, in terms of labour, buildings and machinery, British farmers are thought to lay out about a third more in such costs than Belgian or Dutch farmers. The British farmer has certainly invested heavily in buildings and machinery, but he is still encumbered with relatively high labour costs, despite the sharp decline in employment recorded since 1950. One reason for the discrepancy is the fairly high incentive income of British farmers, another the larger proportion of full-time employment in terms of output than in the residual peasant regimes of the Continent. Difficulties of interpretation have made these findings contentious, since they challenge the common opinion of the superior efficiency of British agriculture. In detail the calculations may indeed be questionable, but they are sufficiently consistent to suggest that the farmers of the Low Countries and Denmark regularly achieve a better rate of return on their inputs of capital and labour than their British counterparts.

Investment

In capital formation the adoption of new machinery and livestock and the construction of steel or reinforced concrete barns and animal houses have been as characteristic of post-war expansion as the eradication of hedgerows and heavy expenditure upon fuel oil, fertilisers, pesticides and feeding-stuffs. The increase in the horsepower available to farmers implies an immense investment in new equipment, electrical installation, implements, tractors, milking machines, pig and poultry units, cattle houses, milking parlours, grain-drying silos, etc. High inputs invariably signify substantial investment, especially if we include, in the definition of capital, materials exhausted within one year's farming, such as seeds, fertilisers and pesticides, all of which have a direct influence upon the volume of reproducible capital formed in agriculture. The most visible, and the most highly productive, types of agricultural innovation have been capital-intensive, at least since the 1960's. Nevertheless the share of gross domestic *fixed* capital formation contributed by agriculture declined more or less *pro rata* with the receding share of agriculture in gross national output until the early 1970's, from just under 5 per cent in the late 1940's to about 3·5 per cent in 1960 and 2·7 per cent in 1970. The 1970's saw a modest increase in this proportion, so that by 1979-80 the percentage of domestic fixed investment formed in agriculture had again risen to 3·5 per cent. These figures exclude the transfer costs of land and buildings, which do not add to the stock of fixed reproducible capital. From year to year there has been some fluctuation, but the trends have been steady in each of the two stages, 1948-70 and 1971–80. However, since agricultural output has generally increased throughout the period, these data of investment require explanation, especially since the record of growth in other sectors of the economy has been much less consistent. Indeed, the increase in the 1970's can be attributed partly to the poor performance of the other sectors, but there was also a substantial real increase in fixed investment. Modernisation often followed belatedly from the extensive restructuring of the industry that began about 1965, and admission to the EEC encouraged farmers to expand or adapt their activity to meet new opportunities. Relatively few new financial incentives were on offer in the 1970's, but agricultural credit was freely available and much sought. Yet the rise of farmers' indebtedness is not a measure of new investment, since credit has also regularly been employed to finance land purchases and even consumption.

To some extent the slow growth before 1970 was more apparent than real, because after the war farmers laid out large sums in the purchase of 'current' capital stocks. Since current capital is consumed within a year, it is a constant obligation upon businessmen to maintain expenditure upon its replacement. After the war demand for all kinds of current inputs — seeds, fertilisers, feeding stuffs — and also for more livestock was unprecedently high. This pattern of spending has continued. Total current investment in agriculture probably tripled between 1950 and 1966, whereas fixed investment merely doubled.

As for fixed investment it is possible to make comparisons with other sectors for the two categories of 'buildings and works' and 'plant and machinery'. Gross capital formation in agricultural buildings quintupled between 1950 (index 100) and 1970 (index 495). The rapid inflation of the 1970's makes comparison difficult, but it is clear that in real terms expenditure on new buildings and repairs (not distinguishable) was considerably greater than in the 1960's, at least until near the end of the decade. In manufacturing industry the index of investment in buildings increased from 100 in 1950 to 381 in 1970. In agriculture there was a significant acceleration in new works after 1957, when the government introduced the Farm Improvement Scheme and grants were made more widely

111

available and more attractive for many long-term projects, buildings, drainage and improvements to farm layouts. Between 1954–56 and 1960–62 gross investment in buildings doubled from £26 million to £53 million per annum. The scheme is still in force in essentials.

Its success is undoubted but needs placing in context. Even in the 1970's farmers were still employing buildings and under-drains constructed before 1914. A survey in Berkshire in 1971 found that one-third of farm buildings dated from 1957 or later, one-third from before 1914 and the remainder from 1914 to 1956. Cursory examination of other districts supports these findings. In Norfolk and Lincolnshire, for example, I have estimated that in the 1940's about 80 per cent of agricultural fixtures dated from before 1914, most of them from before 1880; in the 1970's more than 40 per cent of brick buildings but less than one-fifth of underdrains or of timber, concrete and asbestos buildings were as old. By 1975 at least two-thirds of fixed installations on the principal steadings of farms had been constructd after 1950. On outlying farmsteads the percentage was less, but many buildings in such places were used inter-mittently. One consequence of the building expansion since 1950 has been that farmers now use much more fixed capital that is not fully depreciated than at any period in the past. In this class of capital, modernisation has been highly successful but it has been concentrated on far fewer sites than in the past, which has made possible many economies of scale in fixed investment.

Surprisingly, perhaps, the rate of investment in plant and machinery has been less. Whereas in manufacturing industry such investment increased sixfold between the late 1940's and the early 1970's, in agriculture it barely doubled. In real terms there has been little increase since the late 1950's. Clearly agriculture has made substantial economies of scale in mechanisation. This is apparent in the declining numbers of some kinds of machinery, but it has probably been influenced also by both the greater size of some implements and by their more efficient use in relation to capital costs since the 1950's.

Mechanisation is a complex process. It cannot be discussed entirely in terms of fixed investments, since there have been far-reaching qualitative as well as quantitive changes since the war. The displacement of horses, like the decrease of manpower, clearly illustrates the growing dependence upon capital-intensive methods of production. The technology of implement design has been no less pronounced but raises rather different issues in the economics of mechanisation.

The diminishing importance of the horse is indicated by the fall in numbers. In 1935–38 there were 675,000 farm horses, and still over half a million in 1944–46. A rapid decline set in soon after; by 1954–57 there were fewer than 170,000, and a decade later numbers had become negligible. Obviously the progress of mechanisation did not depend on the fortunes of the cart-horse, for there are machines compatible with horse-power, as nineteenth-century farming attested, but it is nevertheless usual to compare the declining number of horses with the increase in the use of tractors. The acceptance of the tractor, indeed, opened almost illimitable opportunities for further mechanisation, especially after engineers had developed a successful hydraulic linkage cheap enough to attach to small, general-purpose vehicles: in this respect the introduction of the tractor does mark an important turning-point. The tractor, once regarded with suspicion, and often with contempt in the 1920's and 1930's, had come to seem indispensable even on small farms by the mid-1950's. Horse-keeping decayed not only because it was relatively expensive but also because the horse was increasingly perceived to be less versatile and, even, less dependable than the new Fordsons, David Browns and Fergusons on the market from the end of the 1940's. For smaller farmers who had been scarcely influenced by the existence of the tractor before the war, the prodigious success of the Ferguson paraffin or diesel tractors, which were light, manoeuvrable, cheap to run and fitted with hydraulic transmission, was itself a great stimulus to further demand. Ferguson design was imitated by other manufacturers, and at the same time similar improvements to the larger vehicles employed upon extensive arable holdings raised the efficiency and reliability of all tractors. Implements designed for technically advanced tractors were readily available by the end of the mid-1930's. Moreover, the progress of technology, once begun, continued without hiatus for the following three decades as each manufacturer, increasingly also under pressure from oversea competitors, attempted to produce a more versatile, safer, more potent and more sophisticated series of models to capture the increasingly affluent but discriminating agricultural market. The average tractor on sale in 1980 was very much more complex as a piece of machinery than that of 1950, which in turn was a great advance upon 1930. This has not been fully reflected in prices, for until about 1965 the real cost of most kinds of powered farm implements had actually declined since the 1930's. Thereafter, however, costs rose substantially even in real terms, chiefly because the range of accessories on each vehicle became so sophisticated.

In 1938 there were 64,000 tractors in use in Britain, in 1957 416,000 and in 1967 476,000. By the mid-1950's the tractor had spread to most agricultural holdings, but the saturation of primary demand did not materially diminish sales, despite the apparent slow-down implied in the data, because replacement and additional demand were buoyant. It is striking that the horsepower applied in British agriculture continued to rise steeply throughout the post-war period. Thus whereas the number of tractors between 1956 and 1980 rose by 15 per cent, average horsepower increased from 14 to 45. Moreover by the later 1970's the average age of farm tractors was under three years on the larger arable holdings that had always been in the van of progress. Very much the same pattern of diffusion and persistent technological improvement has occurred in the history of the combine harvester, although satisfaction of primary demand was not achieved until the late 1960's.

Post-war tractors, with their hydraulic apparatus, variable-speed drive and flexible suspension, encouraged farmers to acquire new ploughs, harrows, drills, sprayers, waggons, reapers, tedders, hay sweeps, post augers, hedge cutters, hoists and the like. Virtually all the implements in existence as aids to cultivation, harvesting or general management had to be adapted to fit modern tractors in the 1940's and 1950's. The result was a steady growth in sales of such equipment. In the early years many farmers compromised by keeping one or two horses for hoeing, drilling, sweeping hay, etc., while the tractor was reserved for the heavy work. The high cost of this compromise, however, was against it. Farmers unable to purchase the whole range of necessary implements have been able to make use of agricultural contractors, borrow from indulgent neighbours or join a machinery pool. In this indirect way recent technological advances spread far and wide, touching individuals not otherwise receptive to new ideas. Contract hire is especially important, since farmers have been able to call upon this service either for specialist attention — laying drains, cutting or stubbing out hedges, lifting potatoes, spreading muck, etc. — or to get general work of cultivation and harvesting done, since many contractors keep a complete range of agricultural implements for hire.

By the late 1970's annual expenditure upon plant and machinery amounted to £250 million, of which £125 million were laid out on new machinery. A good proportion of the remainder was reserved for depreciation. An annual rate of depreciation of 20 per cent or more, however, is a misleading statistical abstraction. As with buildings, much machinery is used, especially on small farms, that has effectively been written down. One important consequence of the consumption boom in agricultural machinery after 1958, when the government introduced certain grants in order to subsidise purchase, has been a large but not always buoyant second-hand market for almost every kind of machine, since many well-to-do farmers have replaced machinery more frequently than had been the case in the 1950's and therefore provided less affluent landholders with a useful pool of implements. This was another means by which advances in agricultural engineering were spread throughout the industry.

One of the consequences of the great increase in the use of machinery since the war has been heavy consumption of energy. Before the first world war the horsepower applied in British agriculture, often quite literally *horse power*, was less than one unit for each of the 1·5 million employed in farming. Much of the energy expended on the farm was supplied by human beings, who probably contributed two-fifths or more of the megajoules consumed in agriculture. By 1939 about 3 h.p. was available to each man in farming. Forty years later the figure was over 50 h.p., with many farms in excess of 3,000 acres providing over 100 h.p. per head. By the 1950's much the

115

largest proportion of this energy was supplied from hydro-carbon fuels.

Energy consumption in agriculture has recently been subject to adverse comment. In particular the dependence upon oil to produce and distribute foodstuffs has become an element in criticism of the industry from within as much as by interest groups outside. The argument, however, is finely poised. Most agricultural activities produce more energy in megajoules (or calories) than they consume and could indeed easily produce more, for there are many waste products — yard dung, chat potatoes or surplus straw — that could be used for fuel, either direct or after relatively cheap processing on or near the farm. Leaving such potential savings aside, the actual consumption of the nation's energy on the farm was reckoned to be less than 1·5 per cent in the 1970's, and, even after adding the demands made by closely related services wholly dependent upon domestic agriculture, the quantity of energy consumed did not exceed 4 per cent. The whole of the food industry, from primary production through processing to distribution, did not use more than 12 per cent of British energy supplies. The farms which consumed 1·5 per cent of energy in 1977 delivered over 3 per cent of gross national product.

On the other hand the system of food production does have several drawbacks upon efficient energy use. A quarter of the energy supplied to agriculture is used to manufacture nitrogen-based fertilisers. There is some uncertainty about the effect of applying purchased fertilisers upon rising yields, but it was reckoned in the 1970's that if arable productivity was two-thirds greater and livestock production a quarter greater than they would have been as a direct result of extensive applications of chemical fertilisers, the costs incurred in high-energy manufacturing were probably higher than the benefits accruing from greater agricultural productivity, not least because the use of chemicals has too often also reduced the farmers' interest in the traditional forms of agriculture, especially rotations. Input-output ratios of energy for arable products have in recent years varied — from crop to crop, from season to season and from field to field — between 1 and 3, so that a major saving in the application of manufacturing would have, and could still, improve the balance considerably unless yields fall dramatically.

Similar problems have affected livestock production. All stock farming is relatively expensive of energy. Thus there is for all farm livestock a negative exchange between energy inputs and outputs. The input-output ratio is very diverse but probably averages -6 to -7 for all products except beef, for which about sixteen units of food and other energy are required to produce one unit of digestible energy. The comparative inefficiency of pastoral husbandry, however, extends into simple grazing, so is not merely the result of intensive procedures. There is at least as great a gap between arable crops and pastoral products per acre of cultivated land in terms of energy output as there is between comparative outlays on purchased energy. In other words the differences are fundamental. Provided that people prefer pastoral products before arable products in their diet there will remain, as there has always been, a discrepancy between theory and practice in assessing maximum efficiency in agriculture. There are those who object to animal husbandry on economic grounds, but the majority of farmers and their customers have preferred the compromise which in purely agricultural terms has been best adapted to the climate and geology of Britain.

But some unease remains: even farmers have expressed doubts their heavy dependence upon hydrocarbon fuels in achieving high productivity, particularly since the 1973 oil crisis. Modern techniques of production have become not only too capital-intensive but too energy-intensive as well. To judge from the realignment of fields, the striving after a prairie landscape, and the buoyant sales of high-output tractors and other powered machinery since 1973, few practical agriculturists have been persuaded by these arguments. Because the assessment calls into question the whole rationale of modern high-farming systems, it is improbable that agricultural technology can be amended so fundamentally without either a landslip of prices or another upward adjustment of hydrocarbon fuel costs, even though Continental evidence does not support the close correlation of heavy investment with highly efficient output immanent in British conceptions of agricultural progress.

Because agriculture has become largely a capital-intensive industry since the 1950's the costs of the transformation in terms of agricultural income need to be considered. To some extent the change from labour-intensive to capital-intensive could be accommodated in the cost saving achieved through reducing the volume of manpower employed, but the substitution of machines for men is not sufficient to account for the new initiatives in investment since the war. A substantial enlargement of all kinds of reproducible capital formation has taken place beside an increase at least equally large in agricultural investment in the land itself. The momentum of change towards owner-occupation of farm land accelerated after 1940. Thousands of working farmers have succeeded in enlarging or consolidating their holdings by purchase. This, together with their demand for new capital equipment, has had to be paid for by the agricultural sector, directly or indirectly.

The funds available to farmers for investment have been accumulated from several sources. The improved level of farm incomes in the 1940's, maintained or expanded in the following quarter-century, provided part of the resources for investment. No detailed study of reinvestment of profits has apparently been undertaken, not least because the problem is complicated by the tendency among farmers not to keep capital accounts and to make use of surplus profits to service new or old debts. Nevertheless it is known that the purchase of capital equipment, especially machinery, has always been buoyant after profitable harvests when farmers' liquid funds were at their peak. Bad harvests when profit margins were depressed were by contrast inauspicious for the machinery salesmen. But since there have been fiscal incentives to acquire new capital goods during the post-war period, fluctuations in demand explained by seasonal liquidity have been less pronounced than we might expect. In any event the reinvestment of profits was distinctly inadequate to satisfy the need for both land and capital equipment. In addition to the farmers' own resources the improvement grants offered by government, especially after the 1957 Agriculture Act, have been significant in capital formation. The increased rate of building on the farm after 1958 testifies to the important influence of government subsidisation, at least in setting trends. Within the limits set by the Ministry for making improvement grants the contribution by the Treasury has been considerable, since in any financial year after 1958 there was between £75 million and £150 million available for capital projects or long-term improvements.

The purchase of farm land, which has acquired a momentum often independent of other kinds of investment, has certainly been a heavy commitment for farmers with ambitions for expansion. Part of the investment can no doubt be seen as a species of transfer payment within the agricultural sector. Some at least of the traditional landowners sold part of their estates in order to consolidate or reorganise what they retained, and the money raised by sales of land they reinvested in agriculture or estate management. The largest portion of the money laid out by farmers in buying land, however, was apparently lost to agriculture, being used by the sellers to purchase higher-yielding or less troublesome investments. In such circumstances the appetite for land among farmers was something of a burden upon agriculture, even though it is not at all clear how great the net loss to the industry may have been.

From the farmers' point of view the commitment to large capital expenditure could be met only by borrowing. Since the war agricultural credit has probably not been used extensively to maintain consumption by farmers' families. Profitability was generally sufficient to prevent much eating of the seed corn, in contrast to the less buoyant situation of the 1920's. Indebtedness, however, increased significantly in the 1950's and 1960's. Much of the current debt to banks was incurred to smoothe farmers' cash flow across the seasons, but all the banks, together with certain specialist financial institutions, have lent freely to farmers since the war for various capital projects. Bank debts in agriculture increased from £74 million in 1945 to £553 million in 1971 and £1,300 million in 1979, including loans for the purchase of land. Mortgage indebtedness specifically, much of it channelled through the Agricultural Mortgage Corporation, has risen in the same degree. Thus the volume of outstanding debt held by the AMC stood at less than £10 million in 1950, had risen to £75 million in 1964, and by 1978 amounted to £310 millions. These data have provoked some adverse comment, since they suggest that much of the agricultural debt has been accumulated simply to buy land and has thus put pressure upon the social organisation of agriculture by encouraging too much engrossment. More critically, some polemical writers such as Richard Body have asserted that the regime of intervention has gone beyond the protection of farm incomes and food supplies to promote overborrowing by agriculturists. On the other hand, since institutional lenders seem reluctant to forelose upon farmers, and agricultural bankruptcies have been rather less than the average for businesses of comparable size in the past twenty-five years, the adverse consequences of extended credit have not been evident to the farmers themselves.

7 · Manpower: farmers, farm workers and landowners

The economic maturity of the British economy is demonstrated in the small proportion of the total work force engaged in agriculture. About 1950 employment in agriculture, forestry and fishing accounted for about 5 per cent of the whole. During the 1960's the figure fell below 4 per cent and in recent years has declined further to less than 3 per cent. Quite apart from the fact that the United Kingdom, unlike most of its post-war industrial competitors, has had few workers in primary production who could be recruited into manufacturing or services, the low proportion of agricultural employment has meant that productivity in a classically low-yielding sector has been very favourable. An effective switch from primary production into manufacturing, where productivity is traditionally greater, has not been possible. Nevertheless there has been some movement of labour, for the numbers employed in agriculture have halved since 1950, from about a million to less than 500,000 by 1980. At the end of the war agriculture and service trades supporting agriculture dominated the rural population. In the past thirty years the growth of a diversified population in the countryside and the contraction of agriculture have created a new social landscape. The geographer Vince once calculated that rural Britain contained two-thirds of its work force in primary and one-third in secondary and tertiary employment. Yet there are few districts in which the composition implied by these norms of employment is still extant. It is a reasonable inference from the evidence of developing rural industrialisation since the 1950's that the product of most sections of the countryside is now no longer pre-eminently agricultural. On the other hand it would be a mistake to think that agricultural employment is a residual feature prominent only in remote or backward rural districts. The relative density of agricultural employment is often highest on the outskirts of substantial towns, where

121

hobby farming and intensive horticulture are common, so that districts in the Lea valley and south Lancashire contained more 'agricultural' workers in 1971 than central Norfolk or eastern Lindsey in Lincolnshire.

In the division of labour on farms the old distinction between farmers and labourers has become blurred since the 1950's. The manual operations of agriculture require a wide variety of skills that are shared among farmers, their relatives and wage labourers. The functions of farmers, also, are even more distinctively entrepreneurial and managerial than they were a century ago, when the traditional powers of landlords and their agents were still extensively deployed. In addition, government intervention, the activities of Marketing Boards and farmers' lobbies, together with the growing complexity of land policy, have enlarged the sphere for decision-making as well as the administrative work load of farmers. Agricultural employment includes secretarial and managerial as well as manual elements. It is true, however, that farms, even those with large capital resources, tend to be served by a smaller salaried staff than would be regarded as appropriate in manufacturing or commercial companies of comparable size. Similarly, the wage-dependent labour force that was so obvious on the land even in the 1930's has become by contraction of numbers and the redefinition of responsibilities less distinctively identified as a social class. Farm workers have abandoned the use of 'labourer' to describe their occupational status, but they appear also to have discarded much of their radicalism at the same time.

Farmers

The occupational class of 'farmers' is far from homogeneous. The word describes men (and women) who are either tenants or occupying owners of the fixed capital of their enterprises, and also individuals whose employment in agriculture is part-time. Several 'farmers' apparently use the term for social reasons, since they obtain a considerable portion of their annual income from sources outside agriculture. Moreover the conventional classification is residual in another sense. Not all the occupants of landholdings supplying data to the Annual

Returns regard themselves as farmers, being company directors, accountants, lawyers, innkeepers, even civil servants and schoolmasters in the census. In addition, some farmers registered in the census are inactive, being retired or effectively unemployed except as receivers of dividends or rents. At face value, however, the number of so-called farmers in Great Britain remained quite stable at about 260,000-270,000 between the 1920's and 1960's. In the interim census of 1966 there were still more than 260,000, but the number has certainly declined, probably to fewer than 180,000 by the early 1980's, during the past fifteen years. In the same period the number of holdings recorded in the Agricultural Returns also declined, from 406,000 in 1961 to 216,000 in 1981.

A useful method of classifying farms and farmers is to divide them into full-time and part-time. A large number of holdings before the spate of amalgamations in the 1960's, and not a few thereafter, were insufficient to occupy one man for his whole time. Research in the 1960's discovered that about half of all farms provided insufficient work to be managed as full-time enterprises. This was established by estimating the input of 'standard man days'. A holding not providing work for at least 275 s.m.d. per annum was defined as 'part-time,' even though it was obvious that many such holdings were occupied by men who had no other work. In Scotland in 1965-67, for instance, 8 per cent of nominally 'part-time' holdings were really full-time, whereas 3 per cent of 'full-time' holdings were in fact part-time. In England and Wales in 1960, 11 per cent of occupiers of nominally 'part-time' holdings had no other source of income; 42 per cent had other full-time employment and 14 per cent had part-time employment. Subsequent enquiries indicate that, although the proportions have not been constant, the distinction and distribution of full-time and part-time employment among farmers remains an important fact of agricultural life.

The use of a standardised estimate of labour requirements is probably more accurate than impressionistic soundings as a guide to part-time farming, but the 1960 data indicate that the method has resulted in some overstatement. Many farms in the 1950's and 1960's were incapable of providing adequate recompense to their occupants, even though the farmers

123

had no means or no inclination to eke out their agricultural income by any permanent form of by-employment. The true proportion of part-time holdings in England and Wales in the early 1960's may have been between one-third and two-fifths of all farms (or about 80,000) rather than half, although in Scotland most authorities agree that part-time farms account for at least 45 per cent of the whole number.

The incidence of genuine dual occupation, like the system common before the mid-nineteenth century, is not extinct, but it plays a minor theme in the modern symphony of rural social life. The opportunity for men to combine two enterprises sympathetically in an integrated business career has been less than in the eighteenth century, although the new phase of rural diversification after 1945 may perhaps have changed conditions in some villages. Dual occupations combining agriculture and manufacturing are nevertheless uncommon. On the other hand commuter living has offered new scope for non-agriculturists to enter farming in some kind. Hobby farming is more widespread socially and geographically than it was a century ago. It is especially characteristic of upper middle-class professional and business families partly disengaged from urban life. Well-to-do hobby farmers may occupy land in parcels ranging between 25 acres and 500 acres or more. As a rule, however, this kind of holding, although it contributes to agricultural production, may best be described in terms different from those applied to other forms of part-time farming, because most 'hobby farmers' appear to regard agricultural property as an amenity or profitable investment rather than as a way of life, leaving most managerial and many entrepreneurial functions to salaried managers.

Part-time farmers, properly speaking, have been much more likely to hold secondary jobs in related trades or services. Thus, in 1960, 31 per cent of 'part-time' occupants (and 18 per cent of 'full-time' landholders) in England and Wales were classified as employed in other kinds of agricultural work, including wage labour. Numerous farm workers held, and still occupy, smallholdings. There are also contractors, auctioneers, commercial representatives, advisers, men in agricultural service trades; less typical were non-agriculturists with land-holdings in their names.

The regional distribution of part-time holdings does not everywhere follow the expected pattern. In the Scottish highlands crofting inevitably means that most agricultural holdings cannot provide sufficient employment for the occupiers. Over 80 per cent of holdings in northern Scotland are still technically part-time, although there is often much difficulty in finding alternative, supplementary work. In the Home Counties, by contrast, about half the holdings are part-time; between half and two-thirds of holdings are occupied by white-collar workers of some kind, many self-employed. Part-time holdings are rarest in districts best suited to large-scale agriculture, from Aberdeenshire to Suffolk. They are not uncommon around all the larger concentrations of urban population in the West Riding, Lancashire, Cheshire, Staffordshire, Warwickshire, etc., but, outside the highlands, they exceeded two-thirds of all holdings in the mid-1960's in very few counties: Surrey, Glamorgan, Monmouth and the counties of north-west Wales. The decline in the number of holdings since the 1960's has made inroads into part-time farming, but not equal to the total decline, since the chief victims of engrossment in the past twenty years have been the smaller, tradition-bound farmers on full-time but uncommercial holdings. Part-time farmers, as in Germany, have proved more tenacious than the full-time strugglers.

Farmers' incomes are obviously difficult to generalise, since their economic conditions and personal preferences are so varied. A man owning and occupying 3,000 acres of prime arable land is hardly to be compared with another eking out a livelihood on sixty acres of marginal hill land. The different circumstances of farmers are to some extent reflected in the data published by the Farm Management Survey, which takes annual soundings of income from a large and varied sample of holdings sorted into categories by farming type. The information is difficult to compress into a brief *aperçu*. The survey does produce an 'All types' average income which we may use to illustrate trends, but it should be noted that the economic performance of different types often diverged in particular years and that there may be contradictory tendencies at work through several years, changing the economic relationship between dairying and cattle-feeding, mixed farming and specialist corn-growing, or between big and small farmers.

In the late 1930's the average income of a farmer on 150-200 acres, before deducting interest on capital, was only £250-300 (say £175-200 net) or about equal to the earnings of an adult male industrial worker. The FMS possibly exaggerated, for according to the calculation of aggregate farming net income in 1937-38 the average of a full-time farmer was apparently £160 per annum. In 1955-56 the average drawn from the same calculation had risen to £880 when the survey produced an average of £1,278 on a farm of 193 acres. Between 1946-48 and 1956-58 average net farm incomes increased by 45-55 per cent, according to the different estimates of from £600-£750 p.a. to £880-£1,300. In the next ten years the increase was in the same order of magnitude, with the FMS average and the aggregate net income data more or less in agreement at about £2,000 p.a. in 1966-68. Thereafter money incomes began to climb steeply — 1972-74, £6,000; 1977-79, £8,000; 1980-81, £9,500. Obviously, since these data are expressed in current prices, the real increase since the mid-1950's was much less, but if one compares the trend of farm commodity prices, at least until 1970, with these figures for average income it cannot be denied that farmers prospered well for most of the post-war period. Needless to say, the range between richest and poorest even in the Farm Management Survey, which is biased towards the better-off, is wide in every year's statistics. Thus in 1956-57 the largest arable farmers earned £7,700 p.a. and the smallest stock farmers only £315 p.a.

Aggregate net farm income has increased substantially since the 1930's. Moreover the total has in each period been shared among a smaller number of farmers. However, it is not possible to relate the annual return of agricultural *holdings* to these data, because many holdings are either in multiple occupation or are part of extensive farming enterprises, so that we can merely 'guesstimate' the *per capita* figure, as in the table.

One of the greatest changes to have affected the economic position of the occupational class known as 'farmers' in the twentieth century has been the growth of owner-occupation. The proportion of agricultural land owned by individuals or families who also farmed it increased from 15-18 per cent at

Aggregate net agricultural income in the UK, 1937-8 — 1980-81
(£ million): selected years

1937–38	56	1964–65	478
1946–47	101	1967–68	514
1948–49	290	1973–77	794
1951–52	326	1975–76	1,281
1954–55	293	1978–79	1,245
1956–57	317	1980–81	1,005
1960–61	340		

the beginning of the century to about 50 per cent in the late
1950's and 60 per cent by 1980. The process has been considerably assisted by the tendency towards consolidation. Many
surviving estates have certainly rationalised their structure by
amalgamating holdings, but this has been less important as an
influence than the impulse to buy land among practical
farmers. For some the need of more land is managerial: to
extend operations, to improve efficiency of management, or to
tidy up the physical disposition of the holding. For others the
appetite is social: to acquire more real estate for reasons of
prestige or to endow sons or daughters with separate holdings.
And for many the impetus is financial, for there have been
during much of the post-war period advantages in the
purchase of land under mortgage, particularly when, until the
1960's, the price of vacant possession was comparatively
cheap. Buying land, for a well endowed farmer, performs essentially the same function as the company take-over bid, and the
motives seem equally mixed.

The advancing tide of owner-occupation has not reversed the
course of consolidation. It is possible, but difficult to prove,
that the number of individuals holding land has not
significantly declined since the war, owing to the increase in
the incidence of miniature holdings, mere plots or small
cottage holdings too small to be surveyed by the annual
statistics. These, however, are unimportant even in terms of
access to land for would-be agriculturists. In a more conventional sense the size of holdings has at least doubled, on average, since 1950. In the Farm Management Survey, for example,
which has always been biased in favour of larger farms, the
median holding in the sample has grown from less than 160

acres to almost 300 between the early 1950's and the late 1970's. Moreover, holdings are not necessarily equivalent to 'farms'. Multiple occupancy of holdings by a farmer or a partnership has always been important, and it has made a further advance since the 1960's. Thus in a sample of 125 'holdings', so called in the Annual Returns, in east Norfolk in 1978 averaging 380 acres, there were only fifty-nine 'enterprises' — by which is meant individual family, partnership or corporate businesses — and perhaps, eighty individuals to be described as 'farmers'. Although most of the 'enterprises' exceeded 750 acres there were still a dozen occupying fewer than 300 acres, many of which were ripe for plucking by the 'engrossers', since they tended to be occupied by elderly farmers without obvious successors.

This pattern of consolidation is obviously to be found everywhere, although more work distinguishing 'holdings', 'farms' and 'enterprises' needs to be done before a clear national theme with its regional variations can be composed. My own evidence is insufficient to establish that consolidation has been more active on freehold land than on estate-owned tenant farms. It seems to depend very much on the attitude to business of the landowner and his agent. Resistance to gratuitous amalgamation by appetitive farmers is certainly a feature of some estate policies, but there are no *rentier* estates, so far as I know, where no consolidation of holdings has taken place since 1950, and on most the number of tenants (on retained property) has declined by a third or half at least. In several instances the process of consolidation has been a feature of the change-over from *rentier* to in-hand management by landowners, but the greatest solvent has undoubtedly been the frequency of land sales on old estates.

It is obvious from the progress of consolidation that opportunities for recruitment into farming are more limited now than at almost any time in the past. A more or less unrequited land hunger is not a new phenomenon. In previous periods of agricultural buoyancy new entrants into the industry found it difficult to progress up the farming ladder. When land was difficult to sell or to let opportunities were greater, although applicants for farms were generally less numerous and less affluent. But the bearings of social change in agriculture are not easy to take. Little research has been done on the background, patterns of inheritance and mobility of farmers in any period; documentary material is meagre and the oral evidence unsystematic and confusing. It is, however, clear that farmers have formed a relatively closed group during the past two generations. Newcomers have tended to enter at the top, since the tendency to amalgamate smallholdings has been well nigh irresistible. We do not know what part has been played by part-time farming in diversifying the composition of the social group known as farmers. In many cases the two elements have been kept distinct, especially in districts of widespread hobby farming. A survey in 1944 indicated that 81 per cent of the farmers questioned were the sons of farmers and only 7 per cent were recruited from occupations not directly related to agriculture. Moreover, two-thirds of farmers' children over fourteen were either already in farming or intending to enter the profession, but not necessarily as entrepreneurs.

Opportunities for recruitment had not been too adverse in the 1930's. Land was comparatively plentiful and untypically cheap. It was possible then for men 'to come out of nothing' and to rise through the industry to the limit of their ability or access to capital, although in the very difficult trading conditions before 1935 many failed in the attempt. Even so, in a sample of farmers who entered the profession before 1939 and were still in business thirty years later, the individuals who had come from non-farming backgrounds, about a fifth of the total, were nearly all drawn out of compatible occupations — millers, corn merchants, implement dealers, auctioneers, estate agents, veterinarians, and one was the son of a rural clergyman. Several were the sons of farm labourers, one of a miner and another of a railway clerk. There is no correlation between social origin and eventual success; one man who came of a labouring family and had himself begun as a farm worker had acquired holdings totalling over 2,000 acres by the early 1970's. By contrast a small number of successful farmers were the sons of company directors, lawyers and unoccupied persons of wealth, most of whom had first studied agriculture at Cirencester or another college before being entrusted with their farms.

Among post-war entrants the proportion drawn into agriculture from outside has been even smaller. Nine out of ten farmers under forty-five in 1975, to judge from another sample, were sons of farmers and only a third of one per cent were sons of farm workers. The sample obviously excluded hobby farmers, but it is interesting to note that over half the few part-time farmers with *secondary* occupations recorded were also the sons of farmers or farm workers. Holdings occupied on a part-time basis in the sample districts accounted for only about 30 per cent of all holdings, so the pattern may be untypical, but it does seem that the social origin of part-time farmers may still be more diverse than that of full-time ones. More obtrusive is the fact that the farming population has become more concentrated. Fewer families occupied farms in each neighbourhood in 1975 than in 1935 or 1950. In recent years the only extensive creation of new farms has been by existing farmers, to make provision for younger children to strike out on their own. Even the comparatively common biological failure of farming families has not been made good; engrossment of holdings has everywhere been the order of the day. The problem is that the cost of agricultural land has become too great for all but a handful of newcomers to enter farming. The break-up of the large estates has reduced opportunities for able outsiders to gain any footing in modern agriculture, even though landlords had always been hesitant in admitting men without practical experience or capital. The institutional purchasers of land, equally, have preferred established entrepreneurs to take charge of their holdings. Yet there is ample evidence that recruitment into farming could be extended; potential demand for farms, as for managers' situations, has been buoyant since the 1960's.

As for the farmers in business at various periods since the war, their training in agriculture has certainly improved, partly because educational opportunities have been enlarged and partly because efforts at persuading farmers to seek professional training has since the 1930's been comparatively successful. Various kinds of after-school instruction are available, but none discriminates against wage-earners in preference to entrepreneurs in the industry. However, farm institutes and agricultural colleges have attracted would-be farmers rather than would-be farm workers. Farmers' sons and daughters and those whose best propects have been in the profession of farm management, i.e. those without access to capital or hope of tenancy, have provided the *raison d'être* of most college courses. Tertiary education in agriculture, however, has never been regarded by the farming population as indispensable. Many students of farming still learn the trade by direct experience, and there remain traces of the opposition to the very idea of 'book learning' which was strong before the war.

Social surveys in the 1930's and 1940's indicated that formal education after school was rare among farmers, but that pupillage was normal, although for a majority this merely meant that sons learned the state of the art at their fathers' side. A more detailed study by the Manpower Working Group of NEDO in 1972 discovered that only about 10 per cent of farmers had experienced secondary education and that paper qualifications, at least among the self-employed, were not highly regarded. By the late 1960's the number of individuals leaving universities, colleges and institutes to enter agriculture was no more than 2,400, when the annual recruitment of farmers, managers and workers was about 17,000. Day release courses have probably attracted more employed than self-employed personnel, but at the time of the NEDO survey attendance was as high as 11,000 a year.

Educational background is not easy to translate into performance, whether we are discussing agricultural efficiency or participation in spreading information and defending interests. Attitudes, more broadly defined, are much more difficult to treat. Some studies of behaviour in agriculture have suggested that many differences of practice, entrepreneurial decision-making and professional engagement are essentially attitudinal. They go beyond educational achievement, being much influenced by age, inheritance and temperament. A study in Yorkshire in the 1960's pointed up variations of performance which could not be explained in economic or purely objective terms, and Ruth Gasson's work in Kent produced similar results, but in an area less set in traditional ways. On the other hand, objective standards have been imposed in the determination of agricultural efficiency. The pace has been forced by practising farmers quick to absorb new techniques or new ideas. Intervention during and after the war was carried out on behalf of the Minister by such farmers, whose dynamism usually bemused or antagonised the land-holders whose ways they intended to correct. But innovation was difficult to force, since new ideas percolated slowly through the farming population even in the 1950's and early 1960's. In terms of attitude it is possible to classify farmers into the entrepreneurially active and the entrepreneurially passive, but room must also be left for a large middle group, the dedicated followers of fashion, who do not innovate but need little prompting to try out other men's ideas as soon as those ideas have acquired the necessary *réclame*.

Despite the effective singing in unison of the NFU there is much evidence to suggest that farmers do not form a homogeneous class. Britain has no peasantry, even though there are many poor, under-employed farmers. Agriculture has been too various, its social bearings too diverse and its entrepreneurs too few to form a unitary force in an indus-trialised and urbanised society. Except in the political lobby, agriculturists have preserved too much independence and too little spirit of co-operation to counteract the forces tending to dissolution.

Farm workers

At the end of the war there were over half a million full-time employees in agriculture, together with about 100,000 prisoners-of-war and members of the Women's Land Army and 140,000 casual workers. In 1945-47, therefore, over 900,000 were employed in agriculture in each year — a notable increase upon the 1930's. Even so, a potential seasonal shortage still existed, at least until the end of the post-war period of demobilisation and resettlement. During the war the ploughing campaign, as some experts averred, would have been much more extensive had farmers been able to assure themselves of sufficient harvest labour. The trend towards conversion from tillage in the immediate post-war years was also probably influenced by labour shortages and high labour costs.

Directed labour ceased soon after the war. The prisoners-of-war were repatriated or released by the end of 1948 and the Land Army was dissolved in 1950. Other categories of casual labour increased slightly from 140,000 in 1945-47 to 160,000 in 1950-52, and there was also an increase in full-time employment. The rise, however, was temporary. From the early 1950's numbers in each category declined. By 1955-57 total employment was about the same as in 1937-39, though the composition was different, since regular employment had fallen by about 10 per cent whereas casual employment had increased by over 50 per cent. But in terms of standard man-days the decline between 1939 and 1957 was less than 5 per cent. In the next ten years, however, full-time employment fell by a third and casual by a somewhat larger proportion. A significant turning-point occurred in 1967-68, after which the rate of decline became ever more precipitate. By 1970 the total work force had fallen below 350,000 and in 1980 had reached 250,000. Small as this total seems, there is evidence that the decline, although more slowly than in the 1960's and 1970's, is still proceeding.

The distinction between full-time and part-time or casual labour is useful from the point of view of the statisticians of the Annual Agricultural Returns, but it obscures a number of important social differences. Casual labour, for example, includes both regular part-time employment and seasonal employment. In the latter category are workers who contribute to a pattern of engagement that has been long established. Until many of the processes were mechanised, some planting and many harvesting tasks involved the extensive casualisation of labour. Both organised and 'pick-up' gangs of workers, usually women, were engaged in potato planting and lifting, in fruit-picking, in the hop fields, and sometimes in haymaking and corn-gathering. 'Jobbing' — that is to say, work such as hollow-draining, hedge-laying, ditching, etc. — was also sometimes taken on by casual workers, especially on the smaller farms. In recent years, however, such work has also been extensively mechanised. There are few new opportunities for part-time work of any kind. Regular part-time employment has declined less than full-time or seasonal employment, probably because the work requiring manpower has fallen below the standard of a day's employment on very many farms.

Regional variations are significant but they reflect the size distribution of holdings and the difference in emphasis between arable and pastoral enterprises. Thus in eastern Scotland, in Strathmore, Fife and the Lothians, about half of all farms employed regular labour in 1967 and over a quarter of holdings gave work to three or four workers. Even so the size-group in which most holdings were classified throughout Scotland was of enterprises employing but one labourer apiece. Fifty-one per cent of holdings in north-eastern and 29 per cent in south-eastern Scotland were in this category. In England and Wales regional differences were less marked: 34 per cent of farms in the eastern and south-eastern regions, 28 per cent in the western and south-western, but only 16 per cent in Wales, employed full-time labour. In the northern and western regions well over half of holdings employed only one labourer, and even in the eastern and southern regions only about a fifth gave work to three or four men. Fewer than 4 per cent of farms in Great Britain employed more than ten workers. whereas in the eastern lowlands about a fifth of full-time employees were congregated on these very large holdings.

The statistics of post-war employment in agriculture support the opinion, propagated since the late 1950's by the National Union of Agricultural Workers, that the modern tendency to reduce labour had not only brought about an absolute decline in its potential membership but had simultaneously caused a relative decline, since the working environment of an increasing proportion of labourers had become more isolated and less communal than had been the case in the 1930's and 1940's. Recruitment was therefore more difficult and the sustaining influence of shared experience less evident. What is equally true is that the long-standing distinction between employing farmers and wage-dependent labourers has become statistically less clear-cut since the 1950's even though the social differences between the two groups have not visibly narrowed, especially in the arable counties. According to an analysis of the category of 'regular full-time' labour, attempted in 1965, no less than 22 per cent (70,700 in England and

Wales and 10,300 in Scotland) were described as 'relatives' of the employing farmers; moreover the proportion seems to have risen during the next ten years, since numbers have remained fairly buoyant in this segment. Such family labour was common in the pastoral west but even in the arable east accounted for 10-20 per cent of the regular labour employed. Very striking is the evidence in the survey that about 90 per cent of relatives had no contract of hire and were, in a technical sense, unpaid. However, most were sons or brothers not in partnership, whose remuneration was doubtless adequate, even though cases were brought to light of excessive exploitation of captive family labour, chiefly on small, hardly viable holdings where the entrepreneurs were also impoverished.

If we add to the labour of relatives the contribution of the farmers and their wives the proportion of 'standard man-days' provided within the family exceeded 40 per cent in the 1960's and continued to rise into the 1970's until family labour altogether accounted for over half the total. Even in the mid-1960's three-quarters of all labour costs on stock farms derived from the entrepreneurs and their relatives.

Wage rates in agriculture have been subject to regulation since 1924. In 1947, however, the system was reconstructed, when a national Board, like that established in the war, was authorised to continue its work of fixing minimum rates and hours. The new Board did not supplant the old County Committees, but was empowered to override local agreements if necessary. Particular local traditions and arrangements atrophied in the 1950's. Some differences remain, the result of varying proportions of men paid at basic and at skilled rates, or of the differences between pastoral and arable labour requirements. The convergence of wage rates and hours from the old-established regions into a nation-wide system was a deliberate policy, but it was also inevitable given the range of knowledge available to members of the Board.

The Board, as it was set up in 1947, consists of eight representatives of the farmers, nominated by the NFU, eight representatives of the workers, five of whom are NUAW delegates and three are from the Transport and General Workers Union, and five independent members appointed by the Minister, whose purpose in practice has been to act as arbiters of the conflicting claims of employers and employees. Results have been reasonably satisfactory, although the NUAW has at times expressed disappointment at particular annual awards, since its purpose has been to promote agricultural wages up the scale of comparison with other standards of payment. The awards are held to be binding, so that the influences upon the independent members are considerable. The unions have been most successful in raising relative wage rates at times of headlong emigration of the younger agricultural workers in the mid-1950's and early 1960's.

In the 1940's agricultural wages rose substantially. By 1950 wages were almost three times greater, in money terms, than they had been in 1938 for a somewhat shorter week. Industrial wages barely doubled. Most of the increase occurred at the time of direct control under the wartime administration. Since 1948 the unions have been successful merely in holding the relative position achieved before 1947. Throughout the 1950's wage awards were generally equal to other wage increases, so that farm workers continued to receive about 72 per cent of the average industrial wage throughout the decade. With accelerating inflation in the 1960's and 1970's this position has not been held. For ten years before 1965 basic wage rates increased by about twice the rate of general price inflation: in the next ten years wages actually fell slightly behind prices, by which time agricultural wages only equalled about two-thirds of industrial wages. The trend has continued to the present. The gap in earnings between agricultural and industrial workers, which in 1950 was about £2 a week, had by 1970 increased to £10 and by 1980 to £40.

The basic rate of wages is a useful guide for the purposes of historical comparison but it is a minimum for each class of farm worker. Overtime is ubiquitous. Indeed, as the statutory working week has declined from forty-eight to forty hours, so the amount of overtime has tended to increase. In addition many workers have always been paid more than the basic rates, sometimes because local agreements have put wages above the national average, as in the eastern lowlands, and sometimes because of higher rates paid for special skills or duties.

The principal change in the deliberations of the Wages

Board since 1947 has been the acceptance of wage differentials in its recommendations. At the outset the Board's chief task was to establish minima across the country. Some discretion was allowed under the 1947 Act for consideration of special categories among agricultural workers, but for a decade the NUAW was opposed to graduated awards. By 1960, however, the farmers had been won over, the TGWU delegates were enthusiastic and the independent members so fully committed to differentials that the NUAW fell into line. Thereafter graduated scales were recommended as a matter of course. In 1972 the position of the Board was further strengthened when it was authorised to give workers who acquired the necessary qualifications or carried out the required duties the right to enhanced rates of pay. Throughout the Board has followed common practice, at least among progressive, well-to-do farmers, since additional payments for responsibility had always been made in the majority of counties. But the institutional framework, especially after 1972, clarified much uncertainty and encouraged men to seek an external validation of their accomplishments.

Just as farmers were increasingly exhorted to acquire qualifications or take professional instruction from outside the family circle, so the proficiency of farm workers was an object of expert concern in the 1940's and 1950's. Men intending to make a living from the land, employed and self-employed alike, were encouraged to seek training. The farm institutes offered courses appropriate to men and women who would never have the means to become farmers, and day release courses were mounted in many parts of the country. As with the farmers, virtually all the labourers in agriculture had learned their trade on the farm. Most had left school at the earliest date possible. In this respect little changed between the 1930's and 1950's. The exceptions were for the most part men who were subsequently employed as managers.

There was a minority of workers, above all in dairying or specialised stock-keeping, who had paper qualifications even before the war. This proportion slowly increased. Yet in 1970 the mean age of men leaving school was still below fifteen, but almost as many workers (about 10 per cent) as farmers had experienced secondary education. 9·9 per cent of workers then

137

had an educational qualification of some kind and 9·5 per cent an agricultural qualification other than organised farm training. About 40 per cent of all workers in the sample had no recognised form of training whatsoever and 26 per cent only that provided by experience gained on 'the family farm'. The survey also showed that among the younger men and women some kind of objective instruction had been received; few men over forty-five had obtained any formal training; two-thirds of those under thirty had done so.

The formal regulation of wage differentials, together with the concern among employers that their workers should be able to operate complex machinery. promoted this development. For the farm worker the introduction of proficiency tests as a guide to grading was a spur to self-improvement. But they were part of a more systematic approach to on-farm training which was believed to be more suitable than formal tertiary education. Thus is 1954 a three-year Farm Apprenticeship scheme was established, and amended in 1961 to accommodate the new system of wage differentials. The proficiency test was not tied to apprentice-ship but all workers who entered for the test were assessed by neutral observers who set and maintained standards. These schemes were not resounding successes in the 1950's and 1960's when work was plentiful and the idea of a career spent in farm employment not especially attractive to the abler school-leavers who took work on the land. Another consi-deration is the fact that well over half the annual intake of wage-workers into agriculture are the sons or brothers of farm workers brought up in the ways of the farm for better or worse.

Landlords

Before the first world war the long-standing system in which enjoyment of the land was divided between landlords and tenants was still largely intact. Over 80 per cent of the agri-cultural land in Britain in 1914 was possessed by landowners who did not cultivate their estates. The dissolution of the system of great and middle-sized *rentier* estates had begun in the 1880's, but a significant change towards owner-occupancy was delayed until the end of the first world war. Between 1918 and 1948, when a new Agricultural Holdings Act further reinforced the occupiers' rights, a steady transfer from rented to owner-occupied status took place. In 1950, however, 62 per cent of the agricultural area and 60 per cent of holdings were still tenanted: in 1960 the proportions were 51 and 46 per cent respectively; and in 1977, 44 per cent and 37 per cent. By 1982 only one-third of holdings and little more in terms of land were tenanted. Sales of *rentier* estates have given farmers their opportunities, since many landlords offered better terms to sitting tenants and the alternative of falling into another owner's possession has not been attractive. When land prices have ruled low, as in the 1920's and 1930's, farmers have often taken possession of their holdings or acquired additional land to safeguard their way of life. In times of rising land prices and buoyant demand the investment has been justified, either as a long-term capital gain or to keep rivals out of the running.

Existing farmers or those wishing to enter the profession have not been alone in the market for agricultural land. Speculative buying has perhaps been less common since the 1950's than it was before the war, but there are always institutional buyers, pension funds, commercial and industrial joint-stock companies, nationalised undertakings, financial enterprises as well as a few rich individuals willing to invest in farm property. Government departments have also been active in the acquisition of land from time to time, chiefly for purposes other than land management, especially for defence, transport and urban development. No one knows how much agricultural land now belongs to older institutional and private estates and how much to new institutional estates. It is probable that the number of holdings controlled by the traditional landowners has fallen, from two-thirds to three-quarters of the total in 1914, to about a fifth in 1982. One aspect of landownership that is not well recorded — possession of rented farm land by the owners of small-scale, unsettled estates, perhaps to be described as bourgeois land ownership — has contracted less than the share of the greater estates, but it has not been possible to measure it.

Most traditional proprietors of agricultural land are now also owner-occupiers. Great estates managed in the old style survive to a limited extent in most parts of the country, although no private landlord owns as much land or wields as great a social power as his Victorian predecessor. Nearly all entailed estates have been reduced by sales at least of outlying portions of their land. In the 1970's a substantial aristocratic estate contained between 5,000 and 10,000 acres, or about one-tenth of the size such estates attained in the mid-nineteenth century. Many of the so-called traditional estates are often smaller than estates accumulated by practising farmers since the 1920's, which are as a rule cultivated in hand. The comparatively small scale of recruitment into specialised land ownership by individuals since the war has diminished the social, political and economic importance of the group to its lowest point for centuries. More and more of the ancient gentry and nobility have either sold up and sought their living elsewhere, often in the City, or have settled down to cultivate what remains of their land as farmers. The convergence of landlords' and farmers' interests is well shown in the dominant political role of the NFU, in which both social currents have flowed. More strikingly this community of interests is equally well represented in the Country Landowners' Association. Faced with an inevitable contraction in the number of its traditional numbers and in the political influence it could exercise as a residual lobby of the agricultural interest, the CLA changed into a broader-based pressure group representing all landowners, large and small. Apart from its success in co-ordinating landowners' interests in rural recreations, the CLA has settled down essentially into a lobby petitioning government on general issues such as land taxation and tenancy conditions.

Landowners still have responsiblities that go beyond agriculture. A good part of their time is spent in managing woodland and recreational amenities. This is particularly true of the larger estates and is most applicable to those estates in marginal agricultural regions or in areas of outstanding natural beauty. Moreover most substantial estates managed as rural business are owned by families with extensive commercial connections. The appearance of landowners, above all of institutions, whose acquisition of agricultural property is seen as an investment rather than as a way of life, is not a new phenomenon and it is matched by the growing diversification of business interests among existing landlords. On the other hand the role of the estate owner as industrial or commercial entrepreneur, exploiting coal mines, establishing ironworks, building towns like Barrow or Eastbourne, was exhausted before 1914 and has never been revived. There is no clear evidence relating to the flow of investment between commercial activities and agricultural proprietorship since the war, but for many individuals the fees, dividends or profits to be obtained from occupations other than agriculture or land ownership has been a useful addition to estate income. The difficulty lies in attempting to apportion the share of estate capital formation directly to investment originating in commerce or industry. Since landlords can claim grants for many capital improvements to their estates, investment in buildings and drainage has been widespread since the 1950's. There is no clear evidence that the rate of investment or its volume has been greater on estates purchased by financial or commercial institutions. Their interests seem as often to have been in long-term security as in maximum efficiency of production.

The traditional relationship between landlord and farmer no longer applies to any but a handful of their common interests. The legal obligations of the two remain essentially in force but they have been subject to a series of statutory amendments since the 1875 Agricultural Holdings Act in order to weaken the control of the landowner over his freehold in several ways. The 1948 Act was especially far-reaching, for it laid down not only that most established tenants had security of occupation but also that the arbitrators of rent should fix increases with reference to the tenant's actual situation (length of tenure, previous rent and, in practice, even his ability to pay). This so disrupted the landlord — tenant relationship and encouraged sales of land that it was repealed in 1958. The protection of tenure has become so important that a movement of opposition has recently begun to develop among landowners. The latest revision of the law, in 1977, by which tenants may enjoy security of tenure for up to three generation and which limits the landlords' choice of landholder on his estate in other ways has proved particularly contentious. Security of tenure has probably always been more an issue of principle than an obstacle to good relations on the majority of estates. Yet in

141

inflationary times when there is also much land hunger some proprietors have been tempted to remove unwanted tenants. The best cause for dismissal within the law is execrable husbandry, which might be manipulated. One complaint made by farmers' representatives, especially in Wales, is that landowners have been imposing such extensive demands for repairs and maintenance and so strictly supervising agricultural practices, often without cause, that men have been forced to quit. Statutory requirements, by offering protection to landholders, have sometimes worked to their disadvantage, since owners have interpreted their rights more stringently and less tolerantly. The most common reaction to legal restrictions among owners, however, has been to reduce their involvement with tenancy. The premium expected on the sale of land with vacant possession is a reflection of this preference, since few buyers in the land market want to be saddled with tenants. The differential between the prices of land in vacant possession and of land without possession reached its peak in the early 1950's when the 1948 Act was in force, but in general the gap has widened, if not consistently, between the 1930's and 1940's and the 1960's and 1970's, which is one measure of the disadvantages of tenure from the owner's point of view.

Tenancy may have drawbacks, but there are also benefits for some landowners of letting to experienced agriculturists. The law tends to discourage orthodox tenancy, whether leasehold or in letting from year to year, but the owner can circumvent these restrictions by letting for less than a full year, by means of a partnership with the entrepreneur and by resort to new, less binding forms of leasing. Landholding has therefore become exceedingly complex since the later 1950's. Not all land out of tenancy can be farmed in hand. Retired owner-occupiers and many institutional landowners, as well as some of the traditional estates, have preferred to hand over entrepreneurial and mangerial functions to others but not to confer upon them the security of tenure — hence the diversity of new forms of letting. To some extent these devices have been castigated as legal evasion, but, apart from the fact that the law on agricultural holdings has itself become a deterrent to letting land, the schemes have sometimes acquired special merit by satisfying particular needs among both landowners and landholders. Since so many aspects of orthodox land tenure are inappropriate to modern agriculture the new ideas about letting, co-partnership or even 'sharecropping' can be justified without recourse to explanations of legal evasion. The demand for access to farming land has probably never been greater than in the past fifteen years, so any means of satisfying it is worth active consideration.

The economics of managing rented land seldom compares well with farming in hand. Before the war rural landownership was a way of life rather than a business. Until 1939 this attitude may have been appropriate, because the fiscal burdens on land ownership remained quite low and the social prestige of landlordism was still substantial. Nevertheless even in the inter-war years the most successful landowners were renowned for their businesslike appreciation of market or resource opportunities. Easy-going rentiership was much out of joint with the times in the 1950's. Agricultural improvement, as conceived in the 1947 Act, focused upon the farmer, but implicit in the Act and expressed in some of the orders made by the County Agricultural Committees was the notion that the non-occupying landowner might also need encouragement or prodding to modernise his capital or methods of management. A difficulty was that landlordism was rather unpopular after the war, not least among some activists in the NFU. It was apparently held to be anachronistic rather than malignant, but the attitude was still unaccommodating. Rent control tended to work in favour of the landholder, which may have reduced some inflationary pressure upon agriculture, but it also deterred landlords from investment and probably encouraged the sale of rented land. Moreover, landlords sometimes found that their power to manage their own estates was restricted as much by farmer-led intervention in the interests of 'efficiency' as by the Agricultural Holdings Act. Nevertheless landowners did gain something from the period of planned development before 1955, partly by obtaining priority in the queue for scarce building materials and partly as indirect beneficiaries of government production or capital grants to farmers. From the late 1950's the new emphasis upon production grants in the determination of subsidies, and especially the new building grants, benefited landowners even more than in the period of direct controls. Farm building and under-drainage on all kinds of agricultural property increased notably in the fifteen years after 1958.

The landlord's receipts from property ownership cannot be entirely measured in modern conditions by reference to his rental income. Rent, however, remains the most accessible yardstick for gauging the prosperity of land ownership through time. Rent, however, does not reflect the economic return upon property ownership at all accurately. Rent control will obviously distort market values, but probably not more so than the tendency to 'bid up' rental values by competitors for land in periods of acute shortage, or the opposite in periods of general depression.

In the later 1930's rent for agricultural land, excluding rough grazing, was about £1 an acre. By the later 1940's the average level had more or less regained the position of the 1870's, although the increase was only about one-third the increase in capital costs, between 1935 and 1950. During the 1950's the momentum gathered force. The average exceeded £2 per acre in the late 1950's, reached £2·60 in 1961 and doubled in the next five years. By 1970 average rent was over £12 an acre; it surpassed £22 by 1975 and £30 by 1980. Clearly the movement of rent accelerated after 1950 to make up for the deficiencies of the previous two or three decades. Rents lagged behind land prices until the mid-1950's but then rose in at least the same order of magnitude during the ensuing quarter-century. In terms of both capital and wholesale producer prices the returns upon land ownership were unfavourable until about 1960, but thereafter, even in the inflationary decade of the 1970's, they were much more promising. This improvement in the landlord's economic fortunes was due in part to rising demand for access to land, in part to much more effective management by estate agents, who were charged increasingly to maximise the net yield of the real property, and in part to a more acquiescent attitude to *rentier* landowning by officials, arbitrators and the farmers themselves. Nevertheless the proportion of rent which added directly to the income of the landowner himself, about 40 per cent in 1930's, actually declined to less than a third at the end of the 1960's. Taxes, statutory charges, repairs and improvements, administrative costs, all increased in the post-war period. Nevertheless it is virtually impossible to discover what the average net incentive income of *rentier* landowners may have been at any period, because the sources of income, range of outgoings and complexity of the system of accounting cannot be analysed at all precisely.

Landowners remain important as a social group, but their political authority has declined into insignificance since the 1930's. Their role in agricultural development remains considerable, chiefly because they are still responsible for the provision of much of the fixed capital required in farming. It would be fair to state that even on traditional *rentier* estates the landlords' share of fixed investment was not necessarily exclusive. As in the nineteenth century, tenants have been encouraged to erect buildings, lay down underdrains or realign field boundaries at their own expense. Tenants have long been protected by the system of tenant right by which they are recompensed for unexpired improvements.

However, on almost all estates new work is still commonly undertaken by the landlord. Indeed, new building is often a ground for revising rents and can be subsidised as much for estate owners as for farmers. Because farmers have access to government subsidies, to the banks and to such specialist institutions as the Agricultural Mortgage Corporation, the old dependence, both real and apparent, upon the great landed estates has become a minor theme in their lives since the war. A change of some kind would have occurred even without the rapid expansion of owner-occupancy, but it is characteristic of the rural social order in recent decades that many practising farmers can now look former territorial magnates straight in the eye.

8 · The social bearings of agriculture

Rural society has been transformed since the war. Portrayers of the rural scene have often depicted the changes in sombre colours. The amalgamation of farms and the decline of numbers employed in agriculture have altered the balance of social forces in the countryside, for although agriculture remains the most important industry in terms of output, its needs and preferences no longer dominate the economies of villages and small towns, drawing upon a large supporting force of professional men, technicians, tradesmen and labourers. The agricultural support services are still large and buoyant but they no longer control the reins of rural commerce. The service trades, like modern farms, tend to be concentrated in the hands of big enterprises with a regional rather than local network of communications. As marketing has become oligopolistic many of the traditional functions of smaller towns have become moribund in the post-war world. A countryside dependent upon agriculture must have contracted because of these changes. On the other hand agriculture has generally been prosperous since the war and the greater spending power of the farmers at least should have been sufficient to fertilise rural commerce and social life.

Moreover there is a distinct difference in economic well-being on the farm between 1950's and 1960's and the 1920's and 1930's, when the air of depression, particularly in the corn counties, spread over farms and market towns with equal gloom. Many modern writers, it is true, have adopted an elegiac tone in describing the latter-day countryside, but the pre-war essays of Massingham, Scott Watson or A. G. Street were often threnodic, and with more reason: hopelessness was measured in the flight from the land, in dilapidation, dereliction and social deprivation, in near starvation wages and, often, in near starvation incomes for farmers, in the lack of amenity and opportunity within the rural districts. Not everything was so bleak. The decline of the village, headlong at the end of the nineteenth century, was apparently slowed down in the 1920's and 1930's by the spread of road transport. But even this new facility had ambiguous results. The provision of services by motor bus and delivery van tended to ease the escape of countrymen, if not permanently then intermittently, as the amenities of town life beckoned. Village life was less self-contained, but it was also less isolated in the inter-war years.

One of the consequences of post-war depopulation, deplored by Massingham's literary heirs, has been that those recent links in communication have gradually been broken and many undeveloped villages have again become isolated, at least so far as some social services are concerned. But the diffusion of television and the private motor car has meant that the new order has affected certain social groups much more than others. The rising standard of living in general has made its mark on virtually all British villages since 1950; private affluence, except perhaps among the farmers, has not reached the heights enjoyed in suburban communities, but it has resulted in car ownership becoming widespread in the countryside, although this may in part be attributed to the lack of appropriate public transport. The rural poor, however — characteristically the elderly and the unemployed — cannot always, or often, enjoy the benefits of keeping motor vehicles, and their lives have consequently become more circumscribed than in the days when villages were crowded and highly diversified social organisms. It is on grounds such as these as much as for aesthetic reasons that the transformation of rural society since the war is so often deplored. Nevertheless rural Britain, as distinct from specifically urban parts, has always been heterogeneous, and the differences and particularities of communities remain strongly marked, even though the features of their distinctiveness have significantly changed since the 1920's.

Among the most important variables in the changing pattern of rural life has been relative or differential depopulation. The rural exodus of the fifty years before 1910 was not merely repeated after 1945. Some country districts have contracted *pari passu* with the decline of agricultural

147

employment, though they are very few. Most have either maintained their local population or increased it, often substantially. The south and east, and more recently the south-west, have gained most in numbers outside the boundaries of the larger towns; the marginal agricultural districts of the north and north-west have gained least, partly because no alternative to mining and quarrying has been found to revitalise those parts not well suited to tourism. Generally speaking, however, suburbanisation has progressed across the countryside much farther since the war than was achieved in the ribbon developments of the 1930's. The central areas of great cities have been emptied of people, who have moved out to, or beyond, the outskirts. Glasgow, Liverpool, Manchester and inner London have declined by upwards of a quarter since 1951, and many other cities by more than 10 per cent. The 'conurbations' surrounding the greatest cities, however, have lost population to a significantly less extent, save for Greater London, where a policy of far-flung decentralisation of population was carried through after 1945.

Even so, much of the natural increase of populaion together with some of the migration has been accommodated in rural areas. Overspill settlements, new towns, housing developments in villages outside the Green Belt, as well as the *embourgeoisement* of old villages and market towns, have brought vastly greater numbers of people than traditional rural occupations could satisfy. It is barely possible to think of Surrey or Hertfordshire as agrarian counties, although before 1930 they certainly were, as the works of 'George Bourne' upon Edwardian Surrey demonstrate. By the 1950's the Home Counties were thought to form suburbs of London. The frontier of suburbanisation was constantly moving outwards into Sussex, Buckinghamshire and east Kent. Districts differed in the degree of 'dormitory' infiltration and subsidary industrialisation but there were no rural enclaves within fifty miles of the metropolis unaffected by the process.

The work has continued and created even more intensively suburban landscapes in the past twenty years. At the same time the outward thrust of London has overcome other counties; its tentacles reach into Oxfordshire, Hampshire, Suffolk and Norfolk and become entangled with those of

Birmingham, north of Banbury and Aylesbury. The once clear distinction between town and country has become irrevocably obscured. The result is described by sociologists as the 'rural-urban continuum'. Most of England not part of the nineteenth-century industrial landscape nor insulated by bleakness and inaccessibility is now ruri-urban. Nearly all the changes have affected former agrarian districts, for decayed mining or manufacturing villages are less susceptible to development. Even in the Northumbrian coalfield the new towns of Killing-worth and Cramlington, and in Durham the new town of Peter-lee, were laid out on agricultural sites, not by regenerating existing derelict villages.

Urban values permeate the way of life in the majority of the vestigial agrarian districts that remain. Culturally Britain has become essentially homogeneous since the 1930's. The strangeness and diversity of rural life and traditions disclosed by nineteenth and early twentieth-century investigators of country life were no longer apparent by the 1960's except self-consciously in the Celtic rural districts, and the vogue for British 'folk-ways', especially marked among middle-class migrants into the countryside, in the 1960's and 1970's was the product of deliberate fabrication. That is not to suggest that many articulate countrymen did not regret the super-session of traditional practices and beliefs, for much of the revival was aided and abetted by them, but it was possible only to indulge in nostalgia, not to recreate authentic and self-contained rural communities of the kind still familiar to William Howitt or Richard Hurst in the mid-nineteenth century. It is merely another indication of the extent to which agriculture has lost its central importance in the countryside of the twentieth century.

Suburbanisation has been better controlled by planning since the 1940's. The casual sprawl over good agricultural land has not been eradicated, not least because the state of agri-culture seems to have been a less important consideration than other issues related to development, especially in the years of boom from about 1955 to 1975. Building has generally been grouped and regulated in such a way that existing villages or towns have been extended. Only a few new villages have been constructed, although several of the more important 'new towns' of the period were laid out on green-field sites. Planning has depended upon structural considerations, that is to say, local authorities have drawn up schemes for new development or conservation in the light both of population trends and of expected social needs. Some places have been marked for expansion, others for stagnation, ossification or decline, since planning controls can be used to prevent building as much as to promote it. Away from regions of extensive overspill or suburban development rural Britain has been divided into zones of static population and zones of selective impopulation. The differences within counties are not evident in general demographic data. Virtually all counties outside borough boundaries showed a considerable increase of population between 1951 and 1981. The exceptions are old industrial regions such as non-metropolitan Durham or Lancashire, where a more or less stationary total population disguised much internal migration, so that in effect they belong in the same category as Oxfordshire, Wiltshire or Gloucestershire, where both internal redistribution and absolute growth have taken place. The greatest demographic changes have occurred in counties with 'overspill' development, such as Norfolk, Suffolk, Northamptonshire or Shropshire, since new towns tend to distort many characteristics of rural transformation.

Most of the post-war new towns were built on good agricultural land, usually on fresh sites. The impetus to redistribute the urban population, powerful in the ten years after passage of the New Towns Act, was showing signs of slackening when the government got its second wind. Several new towns were designated in the 1960's. Some, like Livingston and Milton Keynes, were laid out on essentially green-field sites, whereas others — Peterborough, Northampton, Ipswich, Swindon — were intended to form extensions of substantial towns already in existence. Few, however, were planned to regenerate run-down industrial areas except through displacement of existing urban populations. Equally characteristic of the period were smaller 'overspill' towns, usually planned and executed by large-town governments for their own people. Such are Thetford, Dereham, Haverhill, Basingstoke, Kirkby, Bishopbriggs, Ponteland, in which all the development was located upon good agricultural terrain. The rage for depopulating overcrowded cities was often mistaken. The old towns declined too fast and too far for the well-being of the local community. As this failing was recognised in the 1970's the long-term plans for overspill expansion were modified, not always to the advantage of the new communities left in a limbo of half-completed planning. Once again agriculture suffered from the vicissitudes of fashion in structural planning, especially when the change of heart was associated with financial stringency.

The impact of the new towns cannot be distinguished from the more general process of 'ruri-urban' development. The new towns obviously fitted badly into the conventional system of husbandry, not least because many established farms were broken up by piecemeal building. In districts where new towns supplemented a long-run trend of suburbanisation the consequences were less serious than in typically rural districts. Thus in Hertfordshire the expansion of Stevenage, Hemel Hempstead, Welwyn and Hatfield was merely a large episode in the steady process of rural urbanisation. Indeed, as the Town and Country Planning Act attempted to ensure, the new towns as such were intended to reduce pressure for development on land outside designated areas. On the other hand, ribbon development and in-filling did not cease as the new towns were constructed, because restrictive planning could not be sustained as the various towns expanded and tended to run together. How far the experience of Hertfordshire or south Essex has differed from that of nineteenth-century regions of extensive urbanisation is not yet wholly clear, but the consequences for agriculture and agrarian society seem to have been very similar. Much land was lost to housing, industrial and commercial construction and recreation; the number of working farms declined sharply; workers in agriculture, including even some former farmers, were drawn into other kinds of employment in the locality; and there was apparently also some migration of agricultural families out of development areas. The change, however, was quantitative rather than qualitative. If we compare the impact of social change caused by rural urbanisation in the south-east of England, it is difficult to find essential differences between Hertfordshire, where new towns were numerous, and Kent, where no formally designated new towns were situated. It is arguable that Stevenage is a better monument to the planner's art than Becontree or Slough, but the process and consequences for agriculture were the same.

Farther afield, however, the social consequences for the agrarian community were usually greater. The development of Northampton, Peterborough and Milton Keynes not only took away good farm land but also altered the social bearings of large adjacent districts. Very large expansions, the doubling or quadrupling of local populations, are the mid-twentieth-century equivalent of Victorian mushroom towns such as Crewe or Middlesbrough. Their effects upon patterns of employment, prevailing wage levels and social expectations have been no less profound. Deeply rural areas are seldom chosen for expansion. Peterborough, a stagnant railway and brick-making city set in a fertile countryside, has been transformed into a major centre of industrial and commercial growth. The long-term result will be to change one of the most agrarian districts of Midland England into one of the least. The frequency of expanded towns in southern Britain means that there is now no dichotomy between rural and urban except in peripheral zones such as Herefordshire or Lincolnshire. An urban axis runs almost continuously along the Thames valley from the Medway to Bristol, another along the Portsmouth road, and a third, with branches, extends from Greater London through the West Midlands into Lancashire. In between is a *mélange* of farms, and villas, factories and commuter car parks, recreational amenities and overblown prairies sown to corn. Yet eastern and southern England are still the nation's granary. There remains much farm land dispersed among the suburban *bataclan.* Encroachment, indeed, was probably exaggerated by geographers and planners until the 1960's, but the threat of bricks and mortar undeniably acted as a spur to higher productivity. Farmers, indeed, were far from unanimous in regretting the creeping affection of town ways. Development land values were attractive to those who wanted quick profits, and the new populations were useful as customers for retail agricultural produce.

Structural planning in the countryside has affected agriculture indirectly. With very few exceptions planning decisions have not interfered with the agriculturists' management of their holdings, nor with landowners' administration of their estates. Agriculture has suffered most from the loss of land to building, but in other respects farmers are relatively free from planning controls, except in conservation areas. But even in the National Parks there are effective limits to what planning may achieve, because the pattern of private property has not been disturbed by the legislation and the Boards of Control have preferred to work with, not against, the existing land users. As for the Green Belts, created from the 1940's to prevent continuous and unrelieved urban sprawl, farmers have also benefited, since extant activities were not subject to interference whereas competitors in land use have been largely eliminated. The weakness of the Green Belt system is that it placed greater pressure even on some Grade I land outside the area of restriction. These are special cases, however.

The chief agricultural consequence of structural planning has been the differential development of rural areas. Plans drawn up to confine development and promote expansion in comparatively small areas of the counties had the effect of fossilising most settlements outside the chosen districts. The decline of some agricultural villages has been allowed to proceed as farming has become more concentrated and capital-intensive. Those places which have been marked for expansion have been nucleated villages or small towns convenient to take some 'overspill' from nearby urban centres or suitable for small-scale industrial and commercial development. The criteria for choice have little to do with agriculture, for not even the superlative quality of land has necessarily held up development when other considerations have prevailed. To judge from the evidence of six published county structure plans in the 1970's, at least three-fifths of the land earmarked for building has been of Grade II quality or better. By-passes and other extensions to the road network have tended to swallow equally sound agricultural land: there are, indeed, instances of second thoughts on proposed routes in which better land has been sacrificed than originally intended on account of public protests at the social disadvantages of the first scheme. If 50,000 acres or more of new land are taken every year for development the loss is absolute so far as agri-

153

culture is concerned, since virtually no derelict building land is ever returned to farming. It is even the case that some land acquired for building but not used is left uncultivated, although the general rule seems to be that farmers are left in possession, even to sow crops, until the deadline for the change of use is attained.

The decline of agricultural employment has not been uniform throughout Britain, but every parish has seen some fall in the stock of houses and other buildings required for agriculture. About two-thirds of agricultural households disappeared in the course of a generation. The disarrangement of village social life was considerable. Schools, shops, public houses, chapels, churches have been closed, bus services and travelling retail rounds have been discontinued, so that the contraction of agriculture has contributed directly to the atrophy of traditional village life. A recession would have occurred without the headlong decline of farm employment, since post-war prosperity changed preferences in the pattern of consumption and lessened the demand for village-bound services, even among the families of farm workers. Planning decisions have tended to concentrate what remains of these social services in areas of expansion, for, although no direct attempt has been made to suppress the services in villages of no growth, they have inevitably declined further in such places than in others of greater diversification.

In most areas part of the losses brought about by agricultural decline has been made up by the settlement, often in redundant agricultural housing, of weekenders, commuters or retired former city-dwellers. Many of these are owners of second homes and not therefore counted in the census, so that village populations, even if they are increasingly part-time, are certainly larger than official data disclose. The interlopers, however, have themselves distorted rural life no less than the decline of agriculture. In certain regions, resentment against such 'outsiders' has become heated. In parts of Wales and Scotland it has become a burning political issue. The chief ground of complaint is that the outsiders take over housing needed to satisfy local demand and force up property prices beyond the reach of those at work in the neighbourhood. Nevertheless it seems fair to point out that much of the accommodation occupied by commuters and part-timers in old rural villages is still surplus to the needs of a receding agricultural economy. Competition tends to be indirect, influencing property values more than availability.

The decline of agriculture as a social force in the countryside did not bring about an equal diminishment of the farmers' influence. The political power of farmers had always seemed greater than it was, because the landed interest had formed a kind of honorific pre-eminence in the political order even after the real power represented by land ownership and social ascendency had passed away. The farmers had basked in the glory of their landlords' prestige, although even in the nineteenth century the farmers' interests had been voiced by men of their own stamp. The comparatively affluent and articulate farmers who came to dominate agricultural lobbies after the first world war remained in command of the lines of communication with politicians and public during the second and in the following years of growth and prospertiy. The effectiveness of agricultural lobbying after 1940 is almost legendary: the NFU for a period before 1960 was almost an equal partner with the Ministry of Agriculture in determining policies. But, as many politicians recognised, deference to the farmers' interests for the sake of expansion was hardly justified by the real power controlled by the agricultural sector even in the late 1940's. To some extent the concessions obtained by lobbying at the national level are mirrored in the influence still exerted by farmers over rural local authorities. There are still numerous landholders among county and district councillors. Not enough is known about the personal circumstances and business affiliations of local authority representatives, and it is therefore not clear whether farmers as such retain any effective dominance. It seems unlikely, for the composition of the increasingly partisan councils has certainly changed as the rural and suburban population has changed. The rural councils, however, have become safely Conservative, and farmers too are now overwhelmingly Conservative. Thus the clash of interests which occurs in other fields trodden by farmers does not often arise in local government. Farmers, in other words, appear to have retained a considerable representation in local government and at the same time to have benefited from the merging of their interests with those of the right-of-centre rural majority.

The fall in numbers of active farmers may have assisted in the consolidation of their local influence. In the nineteenth century landholders were not politically homogeneous. They differed in wealth, status and religious affiliations. The Liberal-voting, quintessentially Methodist farmers who opposed many features of Victorian Toryism made many rural constituencies marginal. They were mostly men of small acreage and modest wealth with little access to the opinion-forming organs of the landed interest, but who could, if they voted at all, make their presence felt electorally at both national and local level. With the decline both of Liberalism and of Methodism their position was weakened even before the spate of amalgamations after the war drove many of the traditional family farmers out of the industry. The process of rural political change towards a more uniform Conservatism has gone furthest in the agricultural heartlands of England. Needless to say, not all farmers are Conservatives, but individual political preferences do not amount to a group attitude different from the prevailing mood. In the late 1940's the Labour Party had hopes of winning over a majority of the farmers to its cause, and a combination of residual rural radicalism and self-interest (originating in the 1947 Agriculture Act) suggested that these hopes were not misconceived; yet they came to nothing. On the other hand, a successful campaign to recruit farmers by the left of the political spectrum would in itself have produced little political advantage even in the 1950's, unless, as some believed, their indirect influence in setting the tone of rural political allegiances could have brought about far-reaching realignment in the 'Tory' shires.

An equally significant event in the process of Conservative consolidation was the decline of 'working-class' radicalism in the countryside. Especially striking has been the collapse of the influence exercised by the NUAW. Farm workers fell in numbers rather more than farmers after 1950, and although union membership held up in proportion to the numbers employed in agriculture the decline was sufficient to reduce political influence in constituencies where the union was well represented. Rural Norfolk, for example, long had a tradition of radicalism dominated by the agricultural labourers and their allies. Even in 1955, when there was a national swing in the general election to the Conservatives of about 2 per cent, the Norfolk constituencies moved in the opposite direction. The marginal political nature of rural Norfolk was proverbial before 1970, after which rural radicalism in the county virtually collapsed. This retreat coincided with a marked reduction in the wage-labour force employed in agriculture from the later 1960's onwards.

Except on specific issues related to agriculture there is no clear evidence of a distinctive agricultural interest in terms of political representation. That is to say, farmers do not as a rule pursue narrow sectional interests, despite their numbers on many councils, and their workers seldom ever have a voice in rural districts. On the other hand radical policies which might undermine the structure and conduct of farming have seldom been introduced either by national or by local governments, and farmers still enjoy several privileges in respect of planning that they would be very reluctant to lose. Nevertheless farmers and landowners are believed by many of those who protest at their activities to have more power, even if it is only delaying power, than they possess.

Criticism of agriculture has been most effectively concentrated upon the issue of 'environmental' damage caused by modern techniques of production. It began very early. The use of chemical fertilisers was first attacked in the 1930's, chiefly by soil scientists or experimental farmers who preferred 'organic' techniques based upon properly ordered rotations. With the much greater variety of inorganic materials available to assist the farmer since the war, the controversy has become more extensive. In the period of austerity and scarcity public criticism was muted, but from the late 1950's the combination of rising productivity and potential over-production offered a new opportunity for the debate to be aired. Three causes converged in the 1960's. First, there was the serious issue of highly toxic pesticides, notably the derivatives of DDT, that had been extensively used to eradicate pests in several branches of husbandry. Secondly, there was an attack upon methods of cultivation which arose partly out of misunderstanding of a scientific report. It was alleged that the use of heavy implements on the land together with the application of organo-mineral dressings was causing damage to soil structure. Thirdly, many observers of the scene were convinced that stock-keeping practices, the use of batteries and forcing-boxes especially, were injurious to animal welfare. There were also objections that feeding-stuffs were 'laced' with too many chemicals to increase the speed of fattening and reduce the risk of infection, without due consideration of their long-term effects.

The touchwood for the conflagration of public, press-led criticism was the publication in 1963 of Rachel Carson's *The Silent Spring*. This book drew a very plausible picture of impending ecological disaster owing to the use by farmers of organo-mineral preparations for dressing the soil or the crops growing in the soil. It was based on American evidence, but struck a responsive chord immediately in Britain. The result was a campaign to restrict several agricultural practices obnoxious to ecologists and conservationists. The government reacted by referring most of the specific complaints to advisory committees whose recommendations were generally accepted.

The most harmful of the toxins then in widespread use were Aldrin and Dieldrin. They were very effective as pesticides but their potency was so great that they wiped out many less noxious creatures at the same time as they removed the pests. Worse, both left persistent toxic traces which caused long-run damage to the food chain and brought death or sterility to many animals not directly attacked by application of the compounds. The Cox Committee, which examined the toxicity of agricultural chemicals, recommended in 1964 that both should be severely restricted in use. It was thought impracticable to prohibit them entirely, since for many specific treatments — for wireworm for example — no equivalent then existed. Later introductions by chemical manufacturers have been presented for authorisation to a standing advisory committee. Not all organo-mineral preparations authorised for use have been uncontested by environmentalists. Some have turned out to be as hazardous as Dieldrin. Agricultural workers have even objected to handling some products for fear of ill health. Moreover, some preparations are prohibited for retail sale but may be bought by agriculturists in bulk. The inconsistency of these decisions has caused dispute, but has been defended chiefly on the grounds that very toxic chemicals are allowed only when other less hazardous preparations are not available. Scientific opinion about the results of using organo-mineral chemicals is divided. The published research is capable of proving either that conditions have not notably improved since 1964 or that the evidence of environmental damage due to agricultural chemistry has been exaggerated. Certainly the more dire predictions of ecological catastrophe have not been borne out: restriction of the most toxic elements in pesticides may therefore have been sufficient, as the Cox Committee implied.

The more precise issue of damage to soil structure developed out of the controversy over organo-minerals. Intensive tillage, avoiding rotations and dispensing with organic top dressings, was repulsive to many articulate people, including some farmers. Publicity for this notion became more widespread when a press account misinterpreted part of the report prepared by another advisory committee, chaired by Professor Wilson, which appeared in 1969. The report suggested that although there was no evidence of long-term damage caused by modern practices of cultivation, there was some risk that on weak soils the substructure might in certain circumstances be impaired. The risk was exaggerated in subsequent discussion and impelled the Ministry to call for further investigation. The result was to reinforce the generally optimistic findings of the Wilson Committee. Twenty-five years of intensive cultivation of the kind described in the 1960's has not brought about diminishing yields and pervasive infestation of the kind prophesied. It is not known whether the indefinite postponement of nemesis has been the result of faulty prognosis or successful adaptation to forestall damage by farmers.

When critics focused attention upon animal husbandry their complaints were expressed more emotionally. Specific grievances and issues of general principle jostled together and diffused the impetus of attack. One of the first complaints referred to the use of food additives that were hazardous for human consumption. The Americans had discovered in the

1950's that antibiotics in animal diets not only warded off disease but also assisted in food conversion. It was clear, however, that by the time the practice had been extensively adopted in Britain its side effects were ominous. Expert opinion was somewhat divided, and the issue remained open for a long period. In 1971 it was decided that all but three antibiotics should be prohibited in animal feeding. Another problem arose with synthetic hormones, also used in animal diets. In this, however, agricultural fashion preceded the official response, since their use had virtually ceased before the Swann Committee reported in 1971. From time to time other points of grievance received publicity, but since the mid-1960's the advisory committees have been sensitive to public opinion and most doubtful materials, if not forbidden, are at least discouraged.

On the larger question of animal welfare the most potent criticism centred upon the system of intensive livestock husbandry using batteries or close-boxes. The battery system was challenged on the grounds that it was unnatural and inhumane. By the mid-1960's there was widespread disquiet and much persistent lobbying by a relentless minority of objectors. The government as usual responded by appointing a committee under Professor F. R. Brambell to investigate the issue. The Brambell Committee reported in 1965. The report made several recommendations about veterinary control of intensive livestock systems, about minimal standards for housing, including battery sizes, and about diet. But the overriding conclusion was that the state of knowledge relating to animal husbandry was inadequate. There was no evidence of widespread 'cruelty' or neglect of animal welfare, but equally there were few standards by which to measure the concepts. The most important recommendation, therefore, was that a standing committee should be instituted to set standards and establish 'codes of practice'. The government, however, refused to finance the scheme, and little has been done to intervene in the farmers' affairs since the 1960's. On the other hand several improvements have followed from the Brambell report, not least because farmers are in business to make profits and it is generally accepted that good treatment is more likely to be profitable than neglect or cruelty in the care of livestock. The essential point of the Brambell Committee's work is that the idea of intensive, enclosed animal husbandry was not descredited: much of the evidence showed that conditions were better than under the old-fashioned 'free range' method. This did not satisfy the committed opponent but it appeased wider public concern and made continuous monitoring of agricultural practices seem unnecessary. The great influx of the urban middle class into the countryside since the 1960's has probably made the opponents' case easier to sustain, but the problem has been to find a suitable cause to bestir public disquiet since the Brambell report was safely shelved in the Ministry.

Both the campaigns against organo-mineral toxins and against 'battery' farming for livestock have continued. The advisory committees were not radical enough for the genuinely committed opponents of modern agriculture, and there have been those who denied the cautious approval of enclosed livestock husbandry expressed by the Brambell Committee. A greater number objected to the failure of either government or the industry to bring about the reforms recommended by the report. Agricultural interests pointed out that farmers were introducing many of the recommendations, often without direction from above, but this seems not to have allayed the fears of the doubters. Late in the 1970's an outcry was raised against intensive pig farming, although the specific grounds for the complaints were not substantiated; but this new offensive awoke a barely dormant revulsion against battery housing for poultry. The issues were complicated by the widespread evidence of overproduction. This was difficult for the farmers to answer, part of their defence in the 1960's having been the necessity of producing sufficient meat and eggs to feed the people, and in the 1970's they were thrown back upon justification by price. Even so, the objective of the animal welfare lobby was not achieved, since 'cruelty' could not be proved against any of the leading farmers whose methods were attacked. Once more, however, the dispute disclosed the immense differences of atttitude between the two sides.

The disquiet over organo-mineral chemicals continued after the intervention of the advisory committees, even though subsequent innovations in the manufacture of pesticides, etc., have been subject to official approval and accreditation. A recent campaign against the weedkiller 246T, which was organised by the trade unions, illustrates the fact that all is not well with the system of testing, although the chief difficulty has been that many harmful effects have not become apparent for long periods.

Farmers are prone to complain that they are constantly being arraigned before public opinion by opponents of one sort or another. There is a sense in which the agricultural lobby sees itself as embattled against social reformers who would take away farmers' privileges and enforce practices upon agriculture that are ecologically or socially rather than economically or managerially determined. In this state of conflict the battle is often moving from one point of dispute to another. Having turned the impetus of one assault, farmers have to confront another from a different direction. This extreme view is hardly justified by the actual state of public opinion according to the findings of more than one poll of attitudes, but the environmentalists have been able from time to time to find issues that have a wider appeal than most of the specific disputes over policy or methods have achieved. The argument over battery farming, perhaps strangely, did not strike the right note to bring in the whole people on the side of the angels. One of the necessary elements in universalising a grievance is widespread public discomfort. For the majority of people, the opinion polls suggest, farming has a 'good image', based not upon knowledge of real conditions in agriculture but in part upon memories of wartime propaganda in favour of food production as a socially desirable end and in part upon a sentimental nostalgia for old-style farming (obviously fomented by television advertising). Thus the technicalities of alleged 'malpractice' by agriculturists are meaningless to the 'man on the Clapham omnibus'. On the other hand, destruction of public footpaths and the inconveniences brought about by ubiquitous straw-burning tend to outrage public opinion. Less certainly the stubbing out of hedgerows and trees and the pollution of leisure amenities, especially watercourses, may also stir up broad-based opposition to farmers in general.

These points of conflict demonstrate that the countryside is not the preserve of agriculturists. Perhaps it never was. The struggle for access to private land by ramblers and anglers from the industrial towns is more than a century old and some of the most serious confrontations took place in the inter-war years. Before about 1950, however, the conflict was different in kind from most recent disputes. In the 1930's, for example, access to farm land could seldom be denied on *agricultural* grounds. The worst excesses occurred when groups of weekend ramblers came up against landowners whose opposition to public admission to their estates rested upon their desire to preserve game or privacy. In arable districts disputes were few, no doubt because farmers had not ploughed up footpaths, many of which were still in regular use, and did not generally turn away orderly ramblers. There was not yet much competition for the resources of the countryside between farmers and leisure-seekers, except in recognised beauty spots.

The amenity value of the countryside became more prominent after the war, partly because the concept was refined in the period when town and country planning was both professionally and politically in the air and partly because the combination of rural diversification of population and agricultural contraction tilted the balance against the priority of the farmers' interests. Moreover, since farmers rather than 'shooting' landowners became the chief adversaries of the environmentalists and the promoters of leisure, even agriculturally justified changes in land use of landscape were open to complaint. Community interests rather than agricultural needs or preferences were repeatedly stressed in the campaigns organised around the issues of footpaths, hedgerows, pollution, etc. On the question of footpaths the problem has for long been enforcement of the law. In law it is difficult to extinguish public rights of way, but virtual disuse after the war allowed landowners, and especially farmers, to obliterate footpaths.

The ploughing of much ancient grassland caused many to disappear. County councils attempted to re-establish all rights of way not formally abolished, often as part of a general campaign in the later 1960's and early 1970's to reclaim forgotten commons. Protests from farmers and landowners often delayed the progress of way-making; stiles and footbridges were not repaired by the owners whose duty it was to keep them in good condition; various ploys were adopted to deter walkers. Only about half the work of identifying and mapping the rights of way has yet been completed and, although some counties have been exemplary in discharging their legal obligation to keep open footpaths and bridle-ways, many have been unable to gain co-operation from landowners or farmers in the reconstitution of disused field paths. One difficulty is that the details are generally left to the parishes, and recalcitrant farmers cannot easily be persuaded to acquiesce in the law by their neighbours. The argument over access to public footpaths is not legal but practical: farmers have not always conceded that an absolute right still exists for strangers to enter their property, on the grounds that many of the paths are not only useless but often unattractive to ramblers. The method of extinguishing such rights of way is cumbersome and when invoked is generally challenged by interest groups opposed to the loss of all manner of common property.

Disputes over footpaths are irritants in the social relations between agriculturists and the rest of the community. They disclose the extent of disagreement which may exist between various interest groups. Much the same contentiousness has characterised the brief history of straw-burning and stubble-burning. As a problem, burning emerged only in the early 1970's and became serious only in years of very dry conditions such as 1975 and 1976. Most farmers have adhered to the practice despite its almost universal unpopularity, partly to rid themselves of a surplus and partly because burning, especially stubble-burning, is thought to aid fertility. The objectors refer to the waste of a useful resource but also complain about the dangers of smoke and the damage caused by fires running out of control. Some kind of crisis appears to have been reached in the late summer of 1983, but it does not seem likely that the practice will be prohibited or even officially curtailed, so further bouts in the contest of wills must be expected.

The list of offences committed by modern farmers against the public could be drawn out to considerable length. Since the contestants on both sides tend to be combative minorities frequently representing no broader interest than their own, the issues on which they have clashed are usually narrow and cavilling. One more serious complaint needs to be mentioned. Water pollution has changed in character since the enactment of legislation to control industrial emissions. In recent decades the rural watercourses have seemed the more vulnerable, and farmers have received the blame for some of this new pollution. Long-lasting chemical substances in dressing land or crops, slurry washing out from stockyards and, to a lesser extent, toxic material carelessly handled on farms have certainly fouled brooks and rivers. The effect is difficult to distinguish from other manifestations of pollution, and, so far as the delicate balance of wild life is concerned, the leaching of nitrates, nitrites and phosphates must be added to other by-products of modern farming already discussed. In this case, however, there is no remedy in modifying the ingredients used in fertilisers, since the offending materials are essential to the purpose. On the other hand, farmers have been accused, especially in the period before the oil crisis of 1973, of using too much 'artificial' fertiliser, because that which is washed away into the rivers is obviously surplus to requirements, since it has not been absorbed by the growing crops. Higher costs and a better understanding of the function of fertilisers have reduced the dangers to wildlife but they still remain and cannot be avoided, short of wholesale conversion to the principle of organic cultivation.

Statistical appendix

1. Agricultural holdings by size: Great Britain ('000)

Size group Acres	1945	1950	1960	1970	Size group Hectares	1980
300+	14.5	14·8	16·5	20·2	100+	38·1
100·300	77·6	77·0	74·2	65·4	40·100	55·2
50·100	70·4	70·0	66·2	52·0	20·40	40·4
Under 50	275·8	285·9	252·2	129·9	Under 20	117·2
Total	438·2	447·6	390·3	267·5		250·9

Source. Agricultural Statistics of the United Kingdom (annual series)

2. Cultivated land, holdings and employment: Great Britain

Three-year Averages	Cultivated land (million acres)		Agricultural holdings	Regular employees	
	Arable	Permanent grass		Full-time	Part-time
1945–47	17·4	11·3	438,600	624,900[a]	155,700[b]
1950–52	17·0	11·8	452,000	641.100[a]	159,300[b]
1955–57	16·6	12·2	440,000	530,500	89,800
1960–62	17·1	11·8	399,000	450,600	72,600
1965–67	17·3	11·0	362,500	343,300	68,900
1970–72	17·0	10·6	261,000	242,000	66,970
1975–77	16·3	9·5	236,000	202,900	67,700
1980–81[c]	16·3	9·6	216,200	164,500	57,600

(a) 'Regular workers'. (b) 'Casual workers'. (c) Two years only.
Source. As table 1.

3. Area and produce of principal crops: Great Britain

Three-year averages	Wheat		Barley		Potatoes		Sugar beet	
	Area (million acres)	Production (million tons)	Area (million acres)	Production (million tons)	Area (million acres)	Production (million tons)	Area (million acres)	Production (million tons)
1945-47	2·2	1·9	2·1	1·9	1·2	8·0	0·4	3·8
1950-52	2·3	2·4	2·0	2·0	1·0	7·4	0·4	4·6
1955-57	2·1	2·7	2·4	2·9	0·8	5·7	0·4	4·8
1960-62	2·0	3·2	3·6	4·9	0·7	6·0	0·4	6·2
1965-67	2·4	3·8	5·6	8·4	0·6	6·5	0·4	6·7
1970-72	2·6	4·4	5·4	8·6	0·6	6·7	0·5	6·8
1975-77	2·7	5·0	5·4	8·4	0·5	6·3	0·5	5·9
1980-82[a]	3·6	8·5	5·6	10·3	0·4	6·3	0·5	7·4

(a) Average of two years only.
Source. As table 1.

5. Prices indices: United Kingdom averages, 1955-81

	Wheat	Barley	Potatoes (maincrop)	Milk	Eggs	Wool	Poultry	Cattle (fat)	Lambs (fat)	Porkers (fat)
1955-57 = 100										
1955	98·1	98·4	104·4	102·4	102·7	100·6	104·8	114·5	99·0	93·8
1956	106·6	100·5	110·0	101·1	98·8	99·1	94·2	88·3	96·9	107·5
1957	91·3	91·6	105·9	94·8	101·7	97·2	96·6	94·7	99·0	100·7
1958	91·2	90·8	161·4	95·9	94·9	92·9	98·2	107·9	100·5	98·4
1959	89·1	86·8	134·9	98·5	84·4	93·3	89·1	115·8	74·0	102·8
1960	89·5	83·7	79·4	93·1	85·3	91·7	87·9	110·0	93·4	109·0
1961	88·2	80·1	106·4	91·6	82·9	91·0	76·0	94·8	71·2	98·7
1962	88·0	86·4	129·1	89·9	77·9	89·8	76·5	108·7	85·2	90·9
1963	84·9	82·8	136·2	92·5	80·6	89·6	75·0	102·0	93·7	96·2
1964	93·0	85·6	106·7	101·0	69·1	93·3	75·9	123·5	108·7	102·5
1965	96·4	90·1	98·4	102·1	74·5	96·6	72·3	132·2	108·3	93·3
1966	96·0	88·5	124·1	103·9	68·2	94·6	72·4	126·8	100·2	114·0
1967	98·2	88·2	131·1	105·9	63·9	93·1	68·4	115·5	99·3	121·1
1968	99·1	89·0	102·1	105·6	68·8	92·6	65·3	143·1	116·3	117·3
1968-71 = 100										
1969	93·1	90·4	105·6	92·5	98·1	102·0	96·4	90·9	103·5	92·0
1970	106·1	112·4	116·2	97·2	99·2	98·8	98·7	93·5	97·3	104·6
1971	101·1	105·5	85·1	107·0	107·8	100·5	107·5	111·5	100·5	99·9
1972	119·1	112·3	100·6	113·2	92·0	102·7	101·7	134·1	138·2	120·4
1973	207·7	194·6	117·4	122·4	153·0	103·5	133·7	175·7	188·7	159·7
1974	252·6	250·8	132·7	151·3	172·4	104·5	173·1	154·8	160·0	165·7
1975	239·6	249·7	305·3	193·4	162·7	126·5	204·8	179·2	195·8	

1975 = 100

1973	86·9	76·2	27·4	63·7	94·0	65·0	88·2	62·4	62·4
1974	103·8	100·4	34·2	79·0	106·1	83·2	79·8	84·6	81·6
1975	100·0	100·0	100·0	100·0	100·0	100·0	100·0	100·0	100·0
1976	131·0	129·1	229·8	117·9	117·9	110·4	128·7	134·2	111·0
1977	146·6	131·5	92·8	128·8	133·2	140·6	147·0	152·3	115·5
1978	154·7	136·0	51·3	133·1	126·3	154·6	168·5	174·0	130·8
1979	166·4	159·1	88·0	142·5	145·1	163·7	186·4	181·8	133·7
1980	172·7	162·0	67·4	161·6	164·0	168·0	195·5	197·8	142·4
1981	188·2	189·1	101·5	177·6	174·5	172·9	216·5	234·4	154·0

Source. As table 1.

4. Livestock on agricultural holdings: Great Britain

Three-year averages	Sheep (million)	Cattle (million)	Dairy cows in milk (million)	Pigs (million)	Poultry (million)
1945–47	18·47	8·68	n.d.	1·61	43·74
1950–52	19·96	9·48	n.d.	3·35	73·91
1955–57	22·86	9·89	2·41	5·07	79·88
1960–62	27·67	10·79	2·60	5·10	98·71
1965–67	28·53	10·97	2·59	6·40	109·73
1970–72	25·03	11·57	2·69	7·38	126·07
1975–77	28·20	11·80	2·70	7·50	128·15
1980–82[a]	30·67	11·76	2·68	7·17	123·26

(a) Average of two years only.
n.d. No information.
Source. As table 1.

6. All products: price indices

(a) England and Wales, 1939·60 (1936·38 = 100)

1939	103	1944	190	1948	249	1953	312	1957	319
1940	143	1945	196	1949	260	1954	310	1958	327
1941	172	1946	207	1950	270	1955	327	1959	317
1942	183	1947	241	1951	296	1956	328	1960	302
1943	187			1952	306				

(b) United Kingdom, 1955·66 (1954·56 = 100)

1955	102	1959	99	1963	97
1956	100	1960	94	1964	98
1957	100	1961	96	1965	99
1958	101	1962	97	1966	101

(c) United Kingdom, 1965·72 (1964·66 = 100)

1965	98.7	1967	102.0	1969	106.1	1971	119.6
1966	101.0	1968	103.2	1970	112.9	1972	127.5

(d) United Kingdom, 1971·81 (1975 = 100)

1971	52.9	1973	72.4	1975	100.0	1977	133.7	1979	152.1
1972	56.3	1974	82.1	1976	128.6	1978	137.8	1980	160.7
								1981	177.9

Source. As table 1.

7. Prices indices of current farm expenditure (selected categories): United Kingdom

(a) 1954-56 = 100

	1954-55	1956-57	1958-59	1960-61	1962-63	1964-65
Feedstuffs	98·4	101·7	90·3	87·2	90·1	96·3
Fertilisers	98·8	100·2	92·3	87·0	86·2	90·4
Fuel	94·7	108·5	104·2	105·7	113·9	117·8

(b) 1964-66 = 100

	1964-65	1966-67	1968-69	1970-71
Feedstuffs	98·5	100·6	104·9	128·2
Fertilisers	95·6	105·1	119·0	130·5
Fuel	96·7	103·3	115·3	125·6
Labour	92·6	106·3	120·8	148·2

(c) 1975 = 100

	1971	1973	1975	1977	1979	1981
Feedstuffs	54·8	79·4	100·0	148·2	163·4	188·1
Fertilisers	44·2	59·3	100·0	118·1	147·2	191·5
Fuel	50·7	54·3	100·0	147·4	181·9	288·5
Machinery	52·8	62·9	100·0	149·8	188·6	234·8
Buildings	52·2	67·0	100·0	137·2	175·3	231·1

Source. As table 1.

8. Annual gross fixed capital formation in agriculture: United Kingdom (£ million at current prices)

	1956	1960	1970	1980
Buildings	27	45	117	535
Vehicles	17	24	18	110
Machinery	50	72	115	399
Total	94	141	250	1,044

Source. Central Statistical Office, *National Income and Expenditure* (annual series).

STATISTICAL APPENDIX

9. Value of gross output and net farm income: United Kingdom
(£ million at historic prices)

	Gross output	Net income		Gross output	Net income
1945-46	625	213	1970-71/1972-73	2,560	650
1951-52/1953-54	1,160	345	1975-76/1977-78	6,012	1,177
1960-61/1962-63	1,594	421			
1965-66/1967-68	1,873	507	1980-81	8,911	1,005

Sources. Output and Utilisation of Farm Produce in United Kingdom;
Reviews and Determination of Guarantees.

10. Share of agriculture in gross domestic product
(£ million at factor cost)

	GDP	Agriculture	%
1950	11,695	682	5·8
1955	16,936	791	4·7
1960	22,405	915	4·1
1965	31,221	1,027	3·3
1970	43,574	1,266	2·9
1975	94,475	2,549	2·7
1980	193,488	4,296	2·2

Source. Central Statistical Office, *National Income and Expenditure.*

11. Percentage of expenditure on various inputs: United Kingdom

	Labour	Machinery[a]	Rent and interest
1938	26·8	9·5	17·8
1946-47	43·4	17·2	10·4
1951-52	30·2	19·7	7·8
1961-62	22·3	16·4	8·7
1966-67	20·4	16·1	10·3
1970-71	19·6	17·4	11·0
1979	20·8	20·9	5·4[b]

(a) 'Machinery' includes both repair and maintenance and depreciation. (b) Interest only.
Source. Calculated from *Annual Reviews and Determination of Guarantees.*

172

12. Machinery employed in agriculture: Great Britain

	Tractors over 10 h.p.	Binders	Combine harvesters	Milking machines
1946	203,500	149,500	20,000	48,300
1954	378,100	142,900	22,400	94,700
1971	405,200	n.d.	62,300	130,800
1981	473,200	n.d.	54,800	66,000 (1977)

n.d. No information.
Source. Agricultural Statistics of the United Kingdom; EEC Eurostat, *Basic Statistic of the Community.*

13. Yields of principal crops: Great Britain

	Cwt per acre			Tons per acre	
	Wheat	Barley	Oats	Potatoes	Sugar beet
1885–89	16	15·5	13	6	n.d.
1925–29	18	16·5	16	6·5	8
1944–46	19	19	16	7	10
1955–57	25	24	19·5	7·5	11·5
1965–67	32	30	25	10·0	14·5
1975–77	36	30	29	9·8	11·8
1980–81	48	36	33	14·2	14·2

Source. Agricultural Statistics of the United Kingdom.

14. Milk and egg yields: Great Britain

	Milk (gallons per location)		Eggs (per bird per annum)
	Per cow	Per dairy cow	
1940	540	n.d.	145
1955	608	691	168
1960	632	768	188
1965	n.d.	798	202
1975	n.d.	902	229
1980	n.d.	1038	248

n.d. No information.
Source. Output and Utilisation of Farm Produce in the United Kingdom (annual series).

15. Livestock: gross output, United Kingdom

Year	Milk (million gallons)	Wool (tons)	Eggs (million dozen)	Poultry (tons)	Beef (tons)	'Sheep meat' (tons)	Pork (tons)
1945	1·75	n.d.	448	n.d.	526,000	132,000	30,000
1955	2·25	51,400	800	180,000	660,000	180,000	460,000
1960	2·62	54,100	1043	300,000	730,000	230,000	790,000
1965	2·44	57,700	1215	410,000	882,000	260,000	920,000
1975	2·93	49,300	1117	650,000	1215,000	275,000	825,000
1980	3·38	51,800	1100	760,000	1191,000	285,000	955,000

n.d. No information.
Note. For poultry, beef, sheep meat and pork the output consists of the weight in 'meat equivalent' values, i.e. including offal and manufactured meat products.
Source. Output and Utilisation of Farm Produce.

16. Self-sufficiency of agricultural production: percentage of consumption

Period	Wheat	Barley	Sugar	Beef	Bacon and ham	Butter	Cheese	Eggs
1936–39	23	46	18	49	29	9	24	61
1945–46	32	93	30	62	38	7	11	44
1953–54	41	67	19	66	43	9	38	80
1960–61	40	82	30	64	33	10	47	93
1969–70	41	90	25	73	37	13	43	99
1974–75	67	102	22	79	n.d.	11	68	99
1980–81	77	114	48	84	n.d.	51	72	99

n.d. No information.
Sources. A Century of Agricultural Statistics: Great Britain, 1866-1966; Eurostat *Basic Statistics.*

17. Consumption *per capita*: United Kingdom

	Liquid milk (pints/week)	*Eggs (per annum)*	*Carcase meat (oz./week)*	*Poultry (oz./week)*	*Bread (oz./week)*
1938	2·99	200	n.d.	0·25	51·30
1955	4·81	227	18·23	0·59	55·10
1965	4·86	249	16·78	3·38	40·60
1975	4·76	215	15·30	5·55	33·67
1980	4·16	192	16·80	6·44	31·10

n.d. No information.
Source. Food Consumption and Expenditure Survey.

18. Basic minimum wages per week: United Kingdom

	Wages (£)	*Average hours*
1945-47	4·03	47·8
1955-57	7·05	47·0
1965-67	10·84	44·1
1975-77	29·70	40·5
1980	70·00	40·5

Source. Ministry of Labour/Department of Employment Gazette.

Guide to further reading

There is as yet no other history of British agriculture since the war, and the treatment in general economic histories has been cursory and superficial, commensurate with the role of agriculture in the modern economy. However, books on contemporary agricultural practice often contain much that is relevant to the history of the subject. The best of these, J. G. S. and Frances Donaldson, *Farming in Britain Today* (Harmondsworth, 2nd ed. 1972), is now somewhat out of date but remains well worth reading. No less judicious is A. N. Duckham, *The Fabric of Agriculture* (1958), and there is a more up-to-date offering by Peter Wormell, *The Anatomy of Agriculture* (1978), which is marred by facetiousness and undisciplined organisation. Geographers have been active in the field since the 1920's. L. Dudley Stamp's *The Land of Britain : its Use and Misuse* (2nd ed. 1950), was a pioneering effort of great importance. Equally significant are J. T. Coppock, *An Agricultural Geography of Great Britain* (1971), and J. T. Coppock, *An Agricultural Atlas of England and Wales* (2nd ed. 1975). F. H. Garner, ed., *Modern British Farming Systems* (1972), is also valuable. E. M. Ojala, *Agriculture and Economic Progress* (Oxford, 1952), was an innovating study in the interpretation of statistics but obviously covers only a small portion of the post-war period. H. T. Williams, *Principles for Agricultural Policy* (Oxford, 1960) is the wide-ranging report of an extensive enquiry into agriculture in the 1950's.

On the role of government, the wartime experience is recounted in detail by K. A. H. Murray, *Agriculture (History of the Second World War)* (1955). A brief but suggestive treatment of post-war trends and problems is by D. K. Britton, 'Agriculture', G. D. H. Worswick and P. H. Ady, eds., *The British Economy, 1945-50* (Oxford, 1952). The best source, especially for the 1950's, is Peter Self and H. J. Storing, *The State and the Farmer* (1962), but I. R. Bowler, *Government and Agriculture* (1979), and H. Frankel, *Economic Change in British Agriculture* (Oxford, 1964), are useful sources of additional information. On support policies see G. McCrone, *The Economics of Subsidising Agriculture* (1962); G. Hallett, *The Economics of Agricultural Policy* (Oxford, 1968, 1979); T. E. Josling and others, *The Burdens and Benefits of Farm Support Policies* (Trade Policy Research Centre, 1972).

Specific economic studies, several intended for undergraduate readers, often range wider than their titles suggest. The following have provided useful information and ideas for the author: E. H.

GUIDE TO FURTHER READING

Whetham, *Economic Background to Agricultural Policy* (Cambridge,
1960); Keith Dexter and Derek Barber, *Farming for Profits* (1967); D.
H. Davey, *Agriculture in the United Kingdom* (Newcastle,1972); D.
K. Britton and B. Hill, *Size and Efficiency in Farming* (Farnborough,
1975); J. R. Bellerby, *Agriculture and Industry Relative Income*
(1956); G. P. Wibberley *Agriculture and Urban Growth* (1959); P. Clery,
Farming Finance (Ipswich, 1975): C. Ritson, *Self-sufficiency and
Food Security* (Centre for Agricultural Strategy (CSA), Reading,
1980); CSA. *National Food Policy in U.K.* (Reading, 1979); CSA, *The
Efficiency of British Agriculture* (Reading, 1980); J. Ashton and A. J.
Rogers, eds., *Economic Change and Agriculture* (1967); A. Edwards
and A. J. Rogers, eds., *Agricultural Resources* (1974); NEDO, *Finance
for Investment* (1975); J. Strak, *The Measurement of Agricultural
Protection* (Trade Policy Research Centre, 1982); G. Sharp and C. W.
Capstick, 'The place of agriculture in the national economy', *Journal
of Agricultural Economics* 17, 1966. On the various aspects of
marketing see G. R. Allen, *Agricultural Marketing Policies* (1959); T.
K. Warley, *Agricultural Producers and their Markets* (Oxford, 1967);
J. J. Davies, *An Enquiry into Methods of Milk Distribution* (HMSO,
1966); *Home-grown Sugar* (British Sugar Corporation, 1961); D. R.
Colman, *The U.K. Cereal Market* (Manchester, 1972); D. K. Britton,
Cereals in the U.K. (1969); M. Butterwick and E. N. Rolfe,
Agricultural Marketing and the E.E.C. (1971); Agricultural Register,
Changes in the Economic Pattern (Oxford, 1957) chs. II-IV; J. Bibby,
The Miller's Tale (1981). For scientific agriculture, Sir John Russell's
A History of Agricultural Science in Great Britain (1966), needs to be
brought up to date. The annual reports of the Agricultural Research
Council are surprisingly useful for the layman, as are many of the
articles in the *Journal of Agricultural Science* (Cambridge, annually).

On the place of Britain in the Common Agricultural Policy, there
are excellent introductory essays by W. G. Jensen, *The Common
Market* (1967); J. S. Marsh and P. J. Swanney, *Agriculture and the
European Community* (1980), and R. Fennell, ed., *The Common
Agricultural Policy: a Synthesis* (Ashford, Kent, 1983). Good
specialised studies include M. Butterwick and E. N. Rolfe, *Food,
Farming and the Common Market* (Oxford, 1968); M. Tracy, ed.,
Prospects for Agriculture in the E.E.C. (Bruges, 1979); Commission
for the European Communities (CEC), *The Agricultural Situation in
the Community* (Brussels, 1974), and *Stocktaking of the C.A.P.*
(Luxembourg, 1975); G. P. Hirsch and A. H. Maunder, *Farm
Amalgamation in Western Europe* (Farnborough, 1978).

No satisfactory study of the farmers has yet appeared. Wormell has
a chapter of limited use on 'The farmers' and Williams deals with
several issues related to recruitment, training and modernisation of
practices. M. C. Whitby, 'The farmers of England and Wales, 1921-
61', *Farm Economist*, II, 1966, and D. K. Britton and K. A. Ingersent,
'Trends in concentration in British agriculture', *Journal of
Agricultural Economics*, 16, 1964, are good survey articles. On parti-

177

cular aspects, Self and Storing are outstanding on the farmers' role in a State-directed agricultural policy, as also is the pioneering report of the Manpower Working Group of NEDO, *Agricultural Manpower in England and Wales* (1972). The Donaldsons' *Farming in Britain Today* has chapters on the small farm problem, which is also dealt with by F. G. Sturrock, *The Optimum Size of Family Farm* (Cambridge, 1945), and F. G. Sturrock and D. B. Wallace, *The Family Farm* (Cambridge, 1956). Ruth Gasson's work is accessible in 'The influence of urbanisation on farm ownership in practice', *Studies in Rural Land Use*, 7, Wye College, 1966; 'Part-time farmers in south-east England', *Farm Economist*, XI, 1966; and on 'Labour' in Edwards and Rogers, eds., *Agricultural Resources*. A. Harrison, *Farmers and Farm Businesses in England* (Reading, 1975); J. Nalson, *Mobility of Farm Families* (Manchester, 1968), and W. M. Williams, 'The social study of family farming' *Geog. Journal*, 129, 1963, offer useful insights and information. Graham Hallett's *The Economics of Land Tenure* (1960) has not been superseded.

For farm workers, Williams and Self and Storing are also useful, but the most comprehensive and interesting study is by Howard Newby, *The Deferential Worker* (1973), a skilful amalgam of sociology and history, which makes the lack of comparable works on the farmers and landowners seem glaring. In addition, F. D. Mills, 'The National Union of Agricultural Workers', *Journal of Agricultural Economics*, 16, 1964; G. H. Peters, 'Capital and labour in British agriculture: a note on productivity measurement', *Farm Economist* II, 1967, and the Economic Development Committee for Agriculture, *Symposium on Agricultural Manpower* (NEDO, 1969), are valuable. For one group, the report by A. K. Giles and F. D. Mills, *Farm Managers* (Reading, 1970), is very illuminating.

Landowning is discussed by Wormell, but the best recent source is D. Sutherland, *The Landowners* (1968). See also A. Harrison and others, *Landownership by public and semi-public institutions in the U.K.* (Reading, 1977); W. Walker-Watson, *The Finance of Landownership* (1954); D. R. Deman, *Estate Capital* (1967).

The debate about agriculture in its social and political context is extensive. Much of the writing has proved to be ephemeral. Journalists have played an important part in stating the 'pros and cons' of agriculture, the agricultural periodicals being especially prompt to defend the farmers' interests against the assault of their opponents or too candid friends. What is easily accessible from thirty years of disputation cannot be described as comprehensive but it is fairly representative of the issues discussed. Several of the general works on agriculture are *parti pris*, notably Tristram Beresford, *We Plough the Fields: British Farming Today* (Harmondsworth, 1975), a lucid apologia for the industry, and Richard Body, *Agriculture: the Triumph and the Shame* (1982), a full-blooded polemic. In the same vein is Garth Christian, *Tomorrow's Countryside* (1966). A selection of books on various ecological questions must begin with Rachel

Carson, *The Silent Spring* (1963), although there are older works of equal importance, e.g. Arthur Howard, *An Agricultural Testament* (Oxford, 1940), and E. B. Balfour, *The Living Soil* (1943). Others to be recommended are Frank Graham, *Since Silent Spring* (1970); Ruth Harrison, *Animal Machines* (1964); J. R. Bellerby, ed., *Factory Farming: a Symposium* (1970); K. Mellanby, *Pesticides and Pollution* (1967); G. P. Wibberley, *Rural Conservation* (1970); T. L. Burton, ed., *Recreation, Research and Planning* (1967); Marion Shoard, *The Theft of the Countryside* (1980); V, Bonham Carter, *Survival of the English Countryside* (1971).

Statistical material is published by many different agencies. For the United Kingdom the *Annual Statistics of Agriculture* issued by the Ministry of Agriculture, Fisheries and Food provide information about cultivation and cropping, livestock, machinery, manpower and (less completely) about productivity. In recent years the same yearbook has given detailed information about product prices and farm costs. The Farm Management Survey produces yearly data on its sample of British farms specifically directed at the financial constitution of participants. The Central Statistical Office publishes annual series of *Abstracts of Statistics* and *National Income and Expenditure*, which include much material upon output, income and factor distribution of the agricultural product. For rents and land prices the *Estates Gazette* and the Institute of Agricultural Economics at Oxford issue annual series. More specialised data are supplied in the Land Classification Survey of the MAFF and in the annual White Paper setting out the government's plans for agricultural subsidisation together with an indication of output, income and price trends ('Review and Determination of Guarantees in Agriculture'). Many other public agencies produce regular series of statistics: the Milk Marketing Board of England and Wales issues *Dairy Facts and Figures* annually, and the Home-grown Cereals Authority, the British Sugar Corporation, the Meat and Livestock Commission, the British Egg Marketing Board (while it lasted), the National Farmers' Union and the National Union of Agricultural Workers have all published valuable statistics. University departments, especially those at Wye College, Cambridge, Newcastle, Oxford and Reading, have also been active in collecting and interpreting data; many of their publications have already been listed above.

The Common Market Commission is another source of first-hand statistics, especially interesting because they are comparative and standardised in form. The annual Basic Statistics should be supplemented by the *Yearbook of Agricultural Statistics* and the monumental *Agricultural Statistics* series (all published in Luxembourg) and by the *General Report on the Activities of the European Communities*, (Brussels, annually). Several UK organisations have also issued Common Market data, e.g. the Home-grown Cereals Authority, *Background to the EEC Cereals Market* (1972); Meat and Livestock Commission, Economic Information Service,

EEC Statistics, 3 vols. (Milton Keynes, 1979), and the Milk Marketing Board, *EEC Dairy Facts and Figures* (Thames Ditton, Surrey, frequent).

Finally a useful source is to be found in the periodicals published for the farming world. Academic journals such as the *Journal of Agricultural Economics* and the *Farm Economist* are indispensable, but rather more entertaining and surprisingly enlightening are the *Farmers' Weekly,* the *British Farmer and Stockbreeder* and *Big Farm Weekly.* Some are given away as free sheets, others sold as conventional special interest periodicals. There is no marked difference in the quality or objectivity of the magazines, which discuss issues in farming politics, usually from the agriculturist's point of view, technical and managerial innovations and practices and offer some insight into the personalities and social profile of the industry. The two largest, *Farmers' Weekly,* which is sold through the usual outlets, and the *British Farmer and Stockbreeder,* the house journal of the NFU, distributed free, have circulations of more than 130,000. At least half a dozen others reach over 25,000 households in each edition, so that the penetration of agricultural journalism through the industry is impressive. Some of the writing is quite distinguished but all deserve the attention of the historian of modern British agriculture.

Index

181